DONALD HUGHES, HEADMASTER

DONALD HUGHES
HEADMASTER

A selection of his writings with a
personal portrait by Percy Heywood

FOREWORD BY
SIR DESMOND LEE

RYDAL

Frontispiece from the portrait by Stanley Reed,
photographed by Ron Rayner

ISBN 0 9501048 0 9
Published 1970 by the Rydal School Endowment Fund,
Colwyn Bay
Copyright © 1970 Rydal School Endowment Fund

Printed in Great Britain by Cox & Wyman Limited,
London, Reading and Fakenham

CONTENTS

FOREWORD

An independent sector in education must never claim to have, and it
would be disastrous if it had in fact, a monopoly of the quality of
independence. But it should be one of its functions to encourage it,
both in the sense of making it possible to do things that would otherwise not be done or not done so well or so easily, and of giving scope
to individuals who might otherwise be cramped, or indeed not survive
in education at all. Whether Donald Hughes would have survived
under the eye, bleak or kindly, of a Chief Education Officer is no doubt
a matter for argument; but he certainly had his full share of the quality
of independence, and in the Schools in which he served scope for its
exercise. Those whose acquaintance with him (like mine) was mainly at
Meetings and Conferences will remember the sharp edge and pungency
of his interventions, not least when debate had become cliché-ridden
or inconsequent. (He did not take Conferences with undue seriousness,
and was as likely to bring his golf clubs as not.) Characteristic was his
address to the Headmasters' Conference in 1964 (included here) in
which he gave the memorable (I have often quoted it) definition of the
Schoolmaster's two temptations as 'the cold shoulder and the hug of
death'. But he was not one who confused originality with breathless
attempts to follow the latest fashion. He could define heresy very
precisely as the over-emphasis of one facet of the truth, and see that the
permissiveness to which all of us (including, as he pointed out, Headmasters) are in these days prone slipped easily enough into the hug of
death. He was too original to be radical. So he cast a satirical eye on the
extremer puffs of the winds of modern doctrine, and if some of what he

vii

said seems almost square, he could show that some of what he criticized (and he was often not entirely out of sympathy with it) approached dangerously near the absurd.

But above all he was a person. Personality is an elusive thing; and one can only hope that what is contained in this volume will convey something of his to those who did not know him, and it will surely recall him to those who did. He was not, he said, a good Committee man; but he was extremely good for those Committees on which he served. He was a Member of the Joint Working Party appointed by the Governing Bodies Association and Headmasters' Conference to report to and negotiate with the Newsom Committee, and for the last two years of his life a member of the Committee of the Headmasters' Conference. Some of us would have welcomed him as a member of that Committee at an earlier stage; perhaps his own diffidence about his capacities as a Committee man prevented it. But some indication of the value his Colleagues placed on him is given by the invitation extended to him to allow his name to go forward for election as Chairman of the Conference for 1968. It fell to me, as Chairman at the time, to convey to him the wish of the Committee and their invitation. The answer was a clear refusal. His doubts about his own abilities and about the amount of travel and absence entailed might perhaps have been overcome; but his doubts about his health and his Doctor's categorical negative could not be gainsaid, and were sadly confirmed by his accident and death. It was characteristic that he described that accident by saying that, feeling unwell, he pulled into a lay-by and 'forgot to stop'. His ability to laugh at all things, including himself, was an integral part of him, and of the affection in which he was held by others.

DESMOND LEE

September 1969

EDITOR'S NOTE

This short Memoir could not have been compiled without great help from many people. Extracts from letters have been freely used, notes written by those who were kind enough to read an early draft proved invaluable, anecdotes and quotes were contributed from a wide variety of sources. To all who helped – too many to list individually – the Editor offers his grateful thanks. The skill and patience of Miss Rosemary Henderson who deciphered the manuscript and typed the drafts demands special mention.

Most of what follows is based on personal recollection and it is therefore all the more appropriate that the Foreword should have been written by Sir Desmond Lee who was able to contribute the 'official' point of view of the Headmasters' Conference. His ready consent to do this was deeply appreciated.

The Rydal School Endowment Fund wishes to place on record its thanks to the Brockhampton Press Ltd of Leicester for its invaluable help in the production of this book.

ACKNOWLEDGMENTS

Permission to reprint the following is gratefully acknowledged.

The Batsman's Bride: *Oxford University Press*
Hymns in School Worship: *Hymn Society of Great Britain*
At a Farewell: *Novello, and the Headmasters' Conference*
Penitence: *Novello, and the Headmasters' Conference*
Neo-Matins: *Prism Publications*
On to Oecumenicity: *Methodist Recorder*
What is Man? *Methodist Recorder*
Retro-Psychoanalysis: *Times Educational Supplement*

Acknowledgments are due to *Riki of Colwyn Bay*
for the photographs reproduced on the following pages
of the illustration section: p 4/5, p. 6 *above*,
p. 7 *left* and *below*, and to the *Yorkshire Post* for the
photograph on p. 6 *left*.

DATES

Born	1911
Entered The Perse School, Cambridge	1921
Entered Emmanuel College, Cambridge	1930
B.A.	1933
Teaching Practice at Whitgift School	1934
Appointed Senior English Master at The Leys School, Cambridge	1934
Appointed Headmaster of Rydal School, Colwyn Bay	1946
President of the Rotary Club of Colwyn Bay	1955–56
Justice of the Peace	1956
Member of the Committee of the Headmasters' Conference	from 1960
Member of the Working Party appointed by the Headmasters' Conference to report to the Newsom Committee	from 1966
Died	1967

Memoir

INTRODUCTION

A formal biography of such an informal person never did seem quite right. A series of 'Tributes' all vying with each other in carefully chosen superlatives would be hopelessly out of tune with the subject. A chapter on Hughes the Christian, Hughes the Headmaster, Hughes the this and that would result in a stuffy portrait which would be a contradiction of the man. Better to let the pen take its own way, guiding only when too scattered a presentation of relevant facts might blur the picture. Whether he would approve of this method is beside the point; he wouldn't in the first place approve of the project but those who knew him well – or little – have a right to be able to be reminded. Those friends of his who were invited to talk about him found considerable difficulty in saying anything and were apologetic for their failure, and it soon became clear that a picture would more easily emerge if the jigsaw pieces were collected and left lying about for each individual to piece together as he or she saw fit. So this is not the definitive biography. If such a thing should exist it may best be found in the extracts here presented from his writings and sermons and speeches. His story is best told in his own words, the interpretation best made by the individuals who read them, leaving the brief episodic memoir as a background commentary.

The selection of his writings which is here presented must inevitably leave out much that might have commended itself to others but too little rather than too much has been the policy and it is hard to believe that the variety and quality of what has been collected does not adequately suggest a whole and vital personality. No attempt has been made to assess him in worldly terms of greatness or success; those who were fortunate enough to come under his influence know that they are the better for it.

'I think,' wrote a friend, 'there must be some emphasis on the effect Donald had on every person and on every gathering however short the contact was.' An obituary notice spoke of 'a rare and splendid spirit whose endearing goodness quickened your own life'. Such a spirit is not to be confined by the words of others. He is his own best advocate.

What follows in this Memoir is based on extracts, sometimes transplanted, from letters and 'Tributes'. All, that is, except for the first three paragraphs and these were written by Donald Hughes himself: they formed part of a review which he wrote of 'The Burning Bow', a selection (with a brief appreciation) of the papers of T. F. Coade, Headmaster of Bryanston. They seemed to form as apt an introduction to this Memoir as could be found.

Chapter 1

*Headmasters and obituaries – 'a supporting kind of person' –
an unconscious evangelist – gaiety of spirit – vocation of teaching
– the life everlasting – one syllable Truths – a balanced
theologian – Lee Abbey and the Church of England –
Christianity inescapable – a great Methodist layman*

'There is a kind of *pietas* which tends to possess writers of the
obituaries of Headmasters, a mixture of nostalgia and charity from
which members of the profession seem to benefit more than most. A
competent administrator who has not done any measurable harm during
his tenure of office too often has greatness thrust upon him retro-
spectively. But great Headmasters are as rare as great anything else, and
no generation is likely to produce very many of them.

'Those who knew him well were assured that if any contemporary
Headmaster qualified for the overworked adjective he was that Headmaster. He had all the qualities that matter – humility, a sense of
humour, vision, faith and, above all, love. He was a man of impressive
integrity, all of a piece, incapable of putting on the sort of flashy public
act which is so common in this day of "Image". To know his personality was to know his character. People speak of his wisdom and understanding, his shyness and diffidence, and his wit. "In him dwelt the love
of God and therefore also the love of man."

'In this time of shifting values and timid abdication from leadership
there are not many authentic prophets in the field of education and to
read his thoughts about Aesthetics and Discipline and Personality and
Responsibility in an educational context is to be inspired and
uplifted.'

He was a person of deep, uncomplicated goodness and an irresistible sense of fun. He had simplicity and this in a man of his intellectual and academic distinction is a rare quality and a great one. It made him accessible, companionable; he was all-of-a-piece,[1] an integrated man. Without saying so he made you realize that the true values in life are the things that are lovely and of good report. 'This is a very difficult time,' he once wrote, 'for the young to grow up in. The standards with which they are confronted are so uncertain and the example of their elders so often shows them very different people from the ones they are supposed to be. They are very good-hearted on the whole but puzzled and their behaviour presents quite new problems at times. We have to be patient and humble with them but we have no right not to be firm.'[2] His innate goodness and spiritual strength must have made him for very many people what Evelyn Underhill has called 'a supporting kind of person'. 'It is hard,' she wrote, 'when these supporting kind of people are withdrawn.'

In his dealings and conversation with all sorts and conditions of men and boys he created the impression of equality. It was one human being talking with another thereby founding and fostering a sense of self-respect and self-assurance in the dimmest and dumbest. Following the Rev. A. J. Costain as Headmaster of Rydal did not make for easy acceptance by the seniors in the School when he arrived; but his immense tact and genuine humility combined with his very real personal interest in individuals 'soon won us round, proud and gauche though we were'.

His courtesy, humour and frank independence made him a fine Christian Apologist – one whose attractive personality was as effective as his words, an unconscious evangelist. He never thrust his faith rudely upon you; he always respected the freedom of others and this in itself was part of his Christian character. In addition to a fine mind and deep conviction he had an aversion from every kind of pomposity and affectation, but perhaps the hallmark of his character was a Christian

---

[1] This is not careless repetition – see page 5.
[2] He once defined tolerance as 'having a mind open at both ends'.

gaiety of spirit. He would quote Wodehouse as effectively as the Bible, as a true Christian humanist. His religion was like his life, practical without ostentation, emotional without sentimentality and his sermons must remain the envy of all who have to preach in school chapels.

As an educationalist he was an expert and a specialist in the field he chose, though the word chose is ill-chosen. School teaching, if it is anything, is a vocation and with him it was in obedience to a call from God; he believed simply that God wanted him to teach, and how right he was. He believed in leaving his staff free to do their own jobs, but he wove a pattern of school life which aimed clearly at the ideals of a Christian community, with respect for the individual and responsibility to the School and to the wider community beyond. He taught and exemplified the Rydal motto: '*Prodesse quam conspici*' and it can be said that no boy passed through the school in his time without being confronted with the virtues of humble and unselfish service to God and man. He spoke and wrote with authority on Education, and a measure of the regard in which he was held by his fellow Headmasters was that many had pressed for his election as Chairman of the Headmasters' Conference. He seemed most obviously qualified for he had the firmest possible grasp of the basic meaning of education, an essential goodness and wholesomeness and an agile mind which, coupled with his kindly but impish sense of humour, would have dealt unequivocally with the trickiest situation. To his fellow Headmasters he seemed to have just about 'all it takes' – a keen and scholarly brain, all the gifts of 'gamesmanship' which would appeal to boys, a fluency of speaking and writing and an easy approach to all men. He was a man for all seasons; a traditionalist without being reactionary; a visionary who had his feet so firmly on the ground that his vision was always practical and practicable.

It was in the later years of school life that his influence really began to lay hold on the ripening mind and spirit, when the irresponsible youth was given responsibility and didn't know what to do with it. In discussions with his prefects 'he seemed to be seeking your advice but was really offering you his'. These were the times when senior boys began to appreciate his true wisdom. During his time at The Leys a

7

generation of boys shared the first experience of war when the sheltered years of youth were abruptly ended with its fears, its insecurity and separations which had never been faced before. In those dark years – and they were dark for him more than for many – he was possibly at his greatest. Many turned to him knowing instinctively that he had a grasp of the countless unknowns which left them baffled and despairing. He summed up his theory of the Life Everlasting in words which have been a help to many:

'God gives us everlasting life. Here we move from the finite to the infinite and since we have only the language of the finite at our disposal it is unprofitable to speculate or to talk too much about it.

'"In my Father's house are many mansions: if it were not so I would have told you. I go to prepare a place for you." That is enough for us. We aren't meant to peer inquisitively into the future, like a weak-minded reader peering into the last chapter of the book and missing the experiences which the author intended for him. Life is to be lived in the present tense; we know enough about the future to live, if we will, in complete trust and confidence.'

The greatest truths, he would say, can always be told in words of one syllable. 'Ye shall know the truth and the truth shall make you free.' He loved to quote this verse not only because it *was* composed of short words but also because it expressed a truth by which he lived.

His theology was marked by a liberalism that avoided on the one side a fundamentalism that offended the Scientific Sixth and on the other the rather vague surmises that marked the 'Honest to God' debate. He had no sympathy with a pale and wistful agnosticism and was entirely devoid of the shallow gimickry of contemporary 'with it' religion. His faith was rugged like the strong mountains. There is nothing in his book on the Apostles' Creed that would offend a middle of the road Anglican; it was indeed his theological balance that made him so refreshing a person in argument and he would undoubtedly have made a great contribution towards Anglican-Methodist Unity. ('It is time we stopped scurrying myopically down the corridors of Time, each clutching our own little bit of Church History.') When presented with the proposition that Anglicanism was a bridge between

Rome and Nonconformity he said that he had always thought of Methodism as the bridge between Anglicanism and the Free Churches. There were those who felt that he himself was that bridge.

Over many years he was a valued friend of Lee Abbey which was founded in 1945 to serve the Christian church as a centre of evangelism and lay training. Although it is an Anglican community it has always enjoyed and encouraged wide ecumenical contacts and Donald had particular links through such long-standing friends as Stanley Betts (formerly Bishop of Maidstone and now Dean of Rochester), Derek Wigram (then Headmaster of Monkton Combe) and Geoffrey Rogers, who was Warden of Lee Abbey from 1950 to 1964.

In October 1965 he was the main speaker at the annual Lee Abbey Reunion in the Westminster Central Hall – incidentally the first non-Anglican to address this gathering of some 2,000 people, so in typical fashion he took the opportunity to welcome everyone to Methodist premises!

In the *Methodist Recorder* of November 1968 there appeared the following letter over the signatures of the Bishop of Coventry, the Dean of Rochester, Derek Wigram and the Warden of Lee Abbey:

'We, the undersigned, recently attended a meeting of the Lee Abbey Council, at which appreciation of the life, and sorrow at the death of Mr Donald W. Hughes, the headmaster of Rydal School, was expressed. This was our first meeting since the Christian cause in this country, from a human angle, had suffered this great loss.

'We should be grateful for the hospitality of your columns to express, from the point-of-view of many members of the Church of England, our deep appreciation of this leading Methodist layman. The fact that his visits to an Anglican Centre have been highlights in our experience will come as no surprise to those who knew him personally. At the time of his death, as a result of a car accident in August, attention was drawn to his brilliant mind and scintillating wit. It is no secret that, had his health allowed, he might well have been Chairman of the Headmasters' Conference. What perhaps has not been emphasized sufficiently is his unusual gift for communicating faith to others, and particularly to the young. His gifted style of writing and gaiety of approach in speaking made those who thought they were opposed ready, at least, to listen. He used to say that he thought he did more for the Kingdom of God teaching English as a Christian, than he did by teaching Divinity.

'While not being a self-conscious ecumenist, he undoubtedly did more than most to help to create an atmosphere in which Christians of differing traditions could find their unity. We would like his Methodist colleagues and those closest to him, to know how greatly he was appreciated by members of the Church of England and how much we, also, shall miss him.'

A man's assumptions are more important than his pronouncements. For that reason he never argued the existence of a loving God: this was axiomatic, what the geometers call 'given'; and for the same reason he could tell mildly irreverent stories of the Deity knowing himself to be entirely on His side and, certain of the integrity of his own faith, he could tell a story about Him that always had an underlying truth. (The theologian asked the computer 'Is there a God?' and received the reply 'There is now'.)

His was no conventional piety – no outworn dogma or untested creed. He ignored neither the intellect nor the spirit, and in faith, reason and imagination lay the rich quality of his life. It was the logic of Christianity that appealed to him – its reasonableness and authentic humanity. He deplored the imbalance between the scientific and the subjective in contemporary culture. 'We human beings,' he said, 'are creatures of two worlds and an enormous amount of the confusion of modern thought has sprung from our failure to recognize this basic fact.' He found Christianity not merely likeable but inescapable. 'The inquiring mind will find a formidable range of intellects ranged on the side of belief in God – (it is not easy to find as impressive a list of sceptics) – but these are the people with whom you must argue if you would prove belief in God to be untenable.'

He was one of the great laymen of the Methodist Church and could have had its highest honours but he was wont to speak teasingly of the office of Vice-President of the Conference, for he set little store by titles and he told his sister that if he were ever to hold such office he would buy her a mink coat. The honour must have come very near and a picture of the cost of the mink coat and the Vice-Presidency being weighed in the balance has a mischievous appeal!

With his death the Christian cause in this country suffered a great loss. He was a man who read the signs of the times aright, and could ill be spared.

'He hath shown thee, O Man, what is good and what doth the Lord require of thee but to do justly, to love mercy and to walk humbly with thy God.'

Chapter 2

As a normal biographer would see it this was an uneventful life. Biographies of Great Men seem to tell of their subjects moving inexorably from this appointment to that, turning aside to sit on a commission or advise on a project in the Antipodes, the whole exercise being freely 'interrupted' by strutting personalities who frequently add nothing to the picture except a sort of bogus distinction. And weirdly fascinating it can be too, even if the list of guests at diplomatic receptions falls short of great prose and the 'dear, witty Noel' sort of catalogue reveals how glitteringly empty great chunks of GREAT LIVES can be.

In this case there is very little to record in the way of historical fact. Donald was born in Southport in 1911 and died in hospital in Hertfordshire in 1967. He was the son of a famous Methodist, Dr Maldwyn Hughes – the last President of the Wesleyan Methodist Conference – before Methodist reunion in 1932 – and he was one of a large, distinguished and devoted family: he had two older brothers and two sisters, one older and one younger than himself. As large families often are, the Hughes were united by the gentleness and strength of their mother, a rare spirit whose character was reflected in the deep concern for people of all ages and which was a mark of all her family. Dr Hughes led the usual peripatetic life of the Methodist minister and between the year of his marriage in 1902 and the comparative stability of residence in Cambridge when he became the first Principal of Wesley House in 1921 the family had had six homes. Not surprisingly Cambridge became HOME and they remained there for sixteen years. Donald laid down roots in Cambridge at that time which he never pulled up and had he lived it is hard to believe that he would have retired to any other part of the country.

His spare time when he was young seems to have been divided between complete absorption in books and marathon cricket matches in which he was Lancashire and his elder brother, Trevor, was Surrey. He was also absent minded enough to go to school one day in two left shoes leaving Trevor to wear two right shoes.

In 1921 he went to The Perse School, an outstanding day school in Cambridge with a staff of personalities and characters (if half the stories Donald told were true). His 'valete' record reads as follows: Head of the School, Captain of West House, Captain of Fives, Hon. Sec. Games Committee, Pelican Rugby Football Colours, School Cricket Colours, 2nd Shooting Colours, Sgt in the OTC, Cert A, 1929, Ex-President of the Union Society, President of the Historical Society, Patrol Leader in School Scout Troop. From The Perse he went in 1930 as a scholar to Emmanuel College and, reluctantly, read Classics Part I. His heart was not in this and after the exams in 1932 he was so certain that he had failed that he asked Trevor to go and look at the results outside the Senate House since he himself could not face the ordeal. He wasn't far wrong either for he got only a 3rd. But immediately he transferred to English the outlook was different and he emerged at the end of 1933 with a 1st. Writing to a friend later he said: 'In Classics I did less well than I had hoped but in English I did rather better than I deserved'. A close friend and contemporary suggests that during his first two years Donald did not really work very hard. Like many others he enjoyed life enormously, belonged to a great many College Societies and played a great many games.

After graduating he took the Teachers' Training Course – Fox's Martyrs they were called, after Charlie Fox who ran the course – spent his term's practice at Whitgift and in 1934 started his career at

The Leys as Senior English Master and House Master of West House.

He remained at The Leys until 1946 and was exiled with the school to Pitlochry from 1940 to 1944 (the Cambridge buildings were taken over by Addenbroke's Hospital), where his only appointment of interest was that of Officer Commanding No. 4 Platoon (The Leys) of the 1st Perthshire Battalion of the Home Guard, a post he held concurrently with that of Battalion Unarmed Combat Officer. (Tell that to the Methodist Conference!) In the latter capacity he toured the Battalion area – most of North Perthshire – with two colleagues from The Leys (the Battalion Intelligence Officer and the Battalion Anti-Gas Officer) giving demonstrations and lectures. Twenty-five years afterwards it is hard to believe that Donald once instructed the Rannoch Section in how to disarm and disable an enemy in the Ticket Office of Rannoch station, a room in which it was hardly possible to stretch one's arms without touching a wall! Those wild days in Perthshire may well have been responsible for the 'fierce' threat which he uttered so often to miscreants that it became a catch phrase; 'I'll kick your teeth in'! In 1945 The Leys returned to their own buildings in Cambridge, but in 1946 on the retirement of Rev. A. J. Costain – a one-time chaplain of The Leys – Donald was appointed Headmaster of Rydal where he remained until his death in 1967.

During his time at Rydal he was gradually drawn into public life. He became a Justice of the Peace, was Chairman of the Colwyn Bay Rotary Club in 1955 and succeeded Rev. A. J. Costain as President of the North Wales Cricket Association. He was a Liberal and took an active part in the Liberal cause (and particularly that of Dr Tegai Hughes) in North Wales; after reading about the antics of some career M.P. he said that the major qualification for entering Parliament should be that you didn't want to. His wise and invigorating interventions on the Headmasters' Conference commended him to his colleagues and he was twice elected to the Committee and subsequently represented the smaller Public Schools on the working party appointed by the H.M.C. and G.B.A. to give evidence to the Newsom Committee. He was a member of the local Hospital Management Committee to which appointment he brought a conscientious if somewhat bewildered sense of duty!

These were the official appointments and relative to those which nowadays threaten to strangle men in 'public life' they constituted an uneventful life. But few people can have had such a full life or such a supremely worthwhile life. Had he never taught English he would have been an outstanding public speaker: had he never spoken in public he would have had few peers as a teacher. Had he never done a day's work in his life but spent his time in 'coffee houses' he would have been a conversationalist of dizzy brilliance. Had he done none of these things he would have been a Methodist minister to rank with the greatest or a Liberal politician who could have doubled the effectiveness of the cause in his single person. But his engagements were of so varied a nature and contracted in such an off-the-cuff manner that they could never be contained in any one category and since he never pursued his reputation they never added up to the image of a public man. An audience at a Cricket Society Dinner at Leeds, a conference of Sixth Formers at Lee Abbey in Devon, an elderly congregation at St John's, Llandudno – these would have only one thing in common, Donald Hughes as principal speaker. And he would move from one to the other with no change of disguise. He never found it necessary to be 'nice' over the tea and biscuits at a Methodist meeting – he simply was nice. He never found it necessary (or possible!) to talk down to a Sixth Form Conference – he was at once on their wavelength and they thereby were on his level. His ready flow of anecdote (shamelessly 'introduced' on occasion) and gracious deprecating manner brought a new touch and distinction to the often 'beery' or 'woolly' after-dinner speeches at cricket or rugby dinners. He never found it necessary to become 'one of the chaps'. There were few who had heard both Sir Norman Birkett and Donald Hughes on cricket who would care to place one above the other.

Though he was no administrator and had brought non-involvement in detail to a permissive art he was paradoxically a splendid committee man for, loathing practical details, he could sort out an intellectual problem point by point with the speed and clarity of a computer, and his heart was so firmly under the control of his head that despite minding enormously about individuals and causes he was able to present his case (and the other too!) calmly and convincingly. And he would do it, of course, with a shaft of wit which would either sugar some debatable pill or burst some bubble of pomposity. (He was pedantic enough in his way to observe and comment on the mixed metaphor.)

Partly because he was a bachelor and partly because he was such a bad organizer he left himself very little empty time and though he generally enjoyed himself when he 'got there' he could, at times, regard his diary with dismay. His public engagements he undertook for various reasons, prominent among them being his indefatigable desire to show the flag; and what Rydal owes to him in numbers of boys who came to the school because he spoke to Rotarians in Liverpool or a Ladies' Circle in Stockport is beyond computation. It would be pointless and individious to indicate the sort of gatherings which he preferred to attend or address. Some must obviously have been simply a chore, some could be taken in the stride and a few were a pure delight for they brought him into a refreshingly different world in which he could perform as the diffident amateur and not be expected to put on the 'professional' act – the Methodist layman or the Educationist – though his amateur act was, of course, pure professionalism.

Within the educational world he was in demand – ever increasing as the word got round – for the pulpit, for the Speech Day platform, for the Teachers' Course, for the Sixth Form Conference, etc., etc. For some extraordinary reason the BBC virtually never approached him and one can only assume that their failure was due to the fact that he never issued a press statement about anything nor wrote a letter to *The Times*. If he did write to the papers it was usually in the form of irreverent verse, poking fun at some political gaffe. One could hardly imagine him writing, 'Dear Sir – May I call attention to, etc., etc.,' or 'I remain, Sir, your most obedient servant, Donald Hughes.' Nor was he capable of viciousness in any public utterance, either spoken or written, though astringency sometimes percolated through. 'Those who can, do; those who can't, teach; those who can't teach do sociology.' Witty, wise and charitable – these were his characteristics and whereas some public figures will address individuals as if they were public meetings, he could hardly avoid addressing a public meeting as if it were an individual. As a result he could at times be disappointing and never more so than when addressing the school on some point of discipline: on such occasions he would merely go through the motions, being either unwilling or unable to simulate passionate indignation or cold anger. Nevertheless, though the immediate impact was not stunning the message itself was usually taken – on reflection. But put him in the pulpit or in his study talking to one boy and the technique (no, that's too calculating a word) was unerring. Conversation, not oratory, was his métier: black and white truths, not purple passages.

As a Rotarian, apart from being Chairman of the Colwyn Bay branch, he was for many years Chairman of International Service, and was in constant demand at Charter Nights; once he even allowed himself to get involved in a Rotary Conference at Blackpool: on his return he confessed to having been as lonely as never before. Not the spirit of Rotary but the genial back-slapping and platitudinous addresses – my words, not his – which are apt to flourish in such gatherings came near to moving him to verse and that was always a sign of mild irritation.

His incursions into the world of cricket dinners, whilst affording him opportunities for playing Rossini rather than Bach, exposed him to the ordeal of listening to the hearty crudities of less sensitive orators whose taste in jokes was more worldly than his own. Embarrassing as these occasions must have been he contrived, through charity, to survive and managed to grow a sort of protective covering, though at the same time he found a connoisseur's delight in the really funny story even if its context and choice of words were of doubtful respectability. Now and then he would report back and re-tell a 'very funny but really most naughty' story from the golf course or cricket dinner.

After he had been at Rydal some years there was a possibility that he might be tempted elsewhere but despite the fact that he gave due consideration to what amounted to an invitation it never seemed likely that he would move. Had he been that sort of person he would have had that sort of life – eventful – but since he was completely lacking in personal ambition as the world knows it he reckoned that the job he was best at was the job he was then doing. In other words he saw it as his duty not to interrupt a mission in one field for a similar mission elsewhere. The cynic may suggest that the upheaval of a move was something that he shrank from but what he declined was what at one time must have surely been his goal. His problem – like his Truth – was really a one syllable one. Could he do a better job elsewhere? If not, why move – except for personal reasons?

A whole Common Room, a generation or two of boys and countless parents and Old Boys sang their silent *Te Deum*.

ABOVE
Donald Hughes

ABOVE RIGHT
Coming out of School

RIGHT
*D. W. H. and
Rev. A. J. Costain
at a rugger match*

ABOVE
At the House Sports

LEFT
Mr and Mrs Costain
at Abersoch

BELOW LEFT
D. W. H. captaining
a Common Room
rugger side

ABOVE
*Golf at Harlech with
Frank Richards*

LEFT
In his study with
The Times *Crossword*

Opening the new Bath

ABOVE
Liberal Rally at Colwyn Bay with Jo Grimond

LEFT
Yorkshire Cricket Society Dinner at Leeds;
left to right,
C. L. R. James,
Sir William Worsley,
D. W. H.
and R. E. S. Wyatt

BELOW LEFT
North Wales Cricket Dinner; left to right,
D. W. H., Ernest Eytle
(W. Indies), P. G. Gadd
(N. Wales C.A.) and
John Cowell (Caernarvon-
shire C.C.)

LEFT
*Speech Day with
Rev. Professor Gordon
Rupp and Mrs K. B.
Jones (Mayor of Colwyn
Bay)*

BELOW
*Speech Day with,
left to right, Sir Arnold
Waters (Chairman of the
Governors), Lord (then
Sir Harry) Pilkington,
Lady Waters,
R. A. Hughes (Mayor of
Colwyn Bay) and Lady
Pilkington*

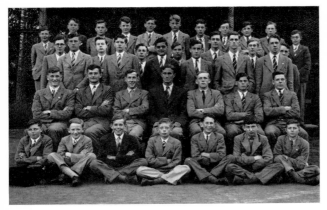

ABOVE LEFT
West House: The Leys
(*at Pitlochry*)

CENTRE LEFT
On a cricket tour
(*in Perth*)

BELOW LEFT
Rydal Dolphins (*in Edinburgh*)

Chapter 3

Personal relationships – Tom Green – Home Guard accident –
the games player – a turning point – the 'pale young curate' –
decision to play golf – on the course

It can be said without fear of contradiction that there was never 'any
woman in his life'. Once, at a Governors' Meeting, reference was made
to certain complications which arose as a result of the Headmaster
being a bachelor. 'No bid,' he murmured to no-one in particular. He
also stated that he never felt he could fairly ask anyone to accept the
position of his 'head'-mistress. Ladies received exactly the same
courteous treatment as men – if they were married the treatment might
be a shade less formal – and if they sometimes thought that he did too
little entertaining they were probably right! Though, as Mrs Sally
Jones his housekeeper extraordinary would testify, there was plenty
going on in term and in the holidays, more often than not, one branch
or other of the Hughes family was in residence. His friends were whoever happened to be around and without deliberate intent he cultivated
no close attachments. He had his golf friends, his friends with whom
he played regular bridge (at one time he was studying Culbertson) and
the four or five friends from Cambridge days with whom every
January he would spend three to four days in unsolemn retreat in a pub
in Sussex; golf would be played and to their great spiritual content
they would then tire the hours with talking. They had discovered the
best possible way of bringing in the New Year.

But no one received special treatment, for all received the best. His
dealings with the Governors although on a more sophisticated level
were indistinguishable from those with a junior boy ('Sir; when's the

whole holiday?' 'Who knows!' 'You do, Sir.') It was simply a question of two reasonable human beings getting together and the assumption of 'office' with its trappings was simply not on. He practically had to be bulldozed into having his portrait painted for the school: on entering the artist's house he was confronted with walls decorated with nudes. 'I'm not being painted like that,' he said. When the portrait was ready for hanging there was quite a discussion in a Governors' Meeting as to how and where it should be hung. 'Over the kitchen sink,' was Donald's contribution. It was strongly urged that it should be hung on the same wall as the portraits of his two predecessors – Osborne and Costain – but he flatly refused to consider the idea, saying that he was not prepared to sit beneath his own portrait while the boys watched him growing old. It was eventually hung on a side wall. Every now and then he made a wan attempt at ceremonial or protocol but almost immediately forgot about it or was so appalled that he abandoned it. Undoubtedly this inability (refusal?) to operate on anything but a man-to-man basis left something to be desired when solemnity was called for. Only once did he seem to come in touch with real anger in front of the school and then it was ice cold and not red hot – intellectual rather than emotional, so to speak.

He could be lonely and would gratefully welcome and seek out company on occasions but seldom seemed to miss particular people – he was always glad to see them – and there was never a suggestion that life was going to be a bit bleak because so and so had gone abroad, etc., etc.; there were so many other people who could fill the gaps and his commitment to any one of them was simply for the duration. In this way he cleared life of much unnecessary emotional clobber and left the intellect free and the spirit unhindered. This accounted a good deal for his equability at all times: more than most people he was able to behave and reason rationally at all times since he bore few of the scars which the more intemperate carry and which under pressure so profoundly affect judgment and poise. Such scars as he had were on a different and deeper level and on the occasion on which they throbbed he found himself in the shadows where no one seemed able to reach him.

There was, however, one friend who merits particular mention for of all people he was probably most able to meet Donald intellectually, spiritually and socially, so to speak. He had much the same impish sense of humour, too. Tom Green, one-time Headmaster of Bootham School, York, was older than Donald by some ten years and died three years before Donald. They had met playing golf at Conway where Tom Green frequently stayed, though he lived in Thornton-le-Dale in the North Riding. Their delight was to talk and play and Mrs Green tells of the perfect day they spent one September which started with 18 holes at Ganton, continued on a sunny afternoon watching cricket at the Scarborough Festival and closed with them falling asleep in their chairs after washing up the supper things spurred on by 'renderings' of 'Throw out the life line', 'Rescue the perishing', 'When the roll is called up yonder', etc. A day, they said, as near heaven as they were likely to get on this earth.

During the war whilst operating with the Home Guard he was given an unhappy opportunity of meeting personal pain and consequent melancholy. On a night operation at Pitlochry he was 'attacking' by crawling up a bank when a defender in pitch darkness let off a 12-bore blank at close range. The wadding of the cartridge went straight into his eye and the eye was subsequently removed. He was in hospital for some weeks at Bangour near Linlithgow enjoying the companionship of a sort of Graham Greene character called Captain Turle whose picturesque speech and single-minded pursuit of nurses and drink was a connoisseur's delight. During convalescence Donald was allowed out to Edinburgh now and then and on one visit saw a play called 'The Duke in Darkness': the fact that it dealt with a character who had his eyes put out entirely failed to quell his delight at the melodramatic and ham-fisted dialogue which might almost have come out of one of his own burlesques.

Before his accident he had played almost all games – except golf. He was a fairly useful performer at all of them but probably less good at cricket – a game at which he would have most wished to excel. But he was an adequate middle order batsman and bowled roundish-arm leg spinners and/or in-swingers. Most of his cricket had been of the 'coarser' variety; long vac sides, scratch teams, the Nondescripts at The

Leys. This Nondescripts side was really his creation and it catered for all sorts and conditions; its standard was usually good village and it travelled much in East Anglia. One of its favourite haunts was Eltisley between Cambridge and St Neots where there is an almost perfect village green ground with thatched roof pavilion, church, etc., etc. For some reason Donald once included Alan Ratcliffe in the side at Eltisley: conditions were hardly calculated to bring out the best in this highly cultured batsman. In the event he was out off a good enough shot caught by someone whom he mistook for a spectator on the grounds that he was wearing braces. How out of touch can you get!

Most of Donald's best cricket was 'played' on Rydal Dolphins' Tours when he would umpire. He was an extremely sound and conscientious umpire and entirely capable of holding his own against Dolphins – batsmen and bowlers – who thought that they were victims of a bad decision. It was very seldom that he missed a school match and he divided his time between a deck chair (with *The Times* crossword) at the far end of Rydal's New Field or a seat on the Pavilion where there was plenty to talk about. But he was fond of umpiring for a couple of hours at half-term: 'they' couldn't get at him at square-leg or at the bowler's end!

He had been a more than useful wing or centre three-quarter and had played regularly for Cambridge Town (City, as it now is): at hockey he was enthusiastic, effective and without style: he was a good tennis and squash player – he had always been light on his feet – and played endless games of both Eton and Rugby Fives. He was a powerful and fast swimmer and was acquainted with the rough justice of water polo. So at the age of 45, minus an eye, there wasn't much left for him to take up except golf; the idea of going for a walk or into the hills never appealed to him in the slightest. Indeed, scenery received only a perfunctory nod as he drove through it; beauty was not to be sniffed at but neither was it to be indulged in for its own sake – it had to serve some intellectual end.

There is a story told of a young ordinand being interviewed by his Bishop's examining chaplain. He was asked what had been his most profound religious experience; this was the moment when he might have recalled with shining eyes his confirmation or perhaps an inspiring sermon by some impressive divine, a vision of something 'out of this world' in Ely or Chartres. But the reply when it came was nothing like that – nor did the Chaplain have long to wait. The religious experience that had meant most to this ordinand was the quite unconscious demeanour of a young master who for one term had happened to sit at the end of his row in chapel at school.

The purpose of quoting this story in this context is not to emphasize the unconscious evangelism of Donald Hughes, though it would serve well, but rather to suggest that not all the great watersheds of experience are marked by impressive cairns. There is some reason to believe that one of the most important decisions in his life was that which determined him to play golf. It was in 1952 after he had been at Rydal for some five years, years which had left their mark on him and caused him to come to the edge of a nervous depression, similar to those which on at least two other occasions caused him to withdraw from his friends.

To set this apparently trivial decision in its context it is necessary to go back some years. When he was appointed Headmaster he had hardly been out of Cambridge. True, The Leys had been evacuated to Pitlochry but it was still a Leysian and Cambridge atmosphere in the school. The family had lived in Cambridge – he had attended The Perse School, proceeded to Emmanuel and then, apart from one term at Whitgift, he had settled at The Leys where he remained until he came to Rydal. He was not – in any sense of the word – a man of the world. Geographically he was as insular as it is possible to be, educationally he had admittedly attended a day school and a resident university and taught at a boarding school but it had all happened in what was, in effect, the sheltered atmosphere of Cambridge. He was indeed extremely inbred and his interests, apart from sport which he played with enthusiasm but never with the skill and absorption of a fanatic – were very largely those of the somewhat earnest (and vulnerable) member of the CICCU[1] and the CSSM[2]. Five years

---

[1] CICCU: Cambridge Inter-Collegiate Christian Union.
[2] CSSM: Children's Special Service Mission.

running he, together with Stanley Betts, helped to run children's missions on the beach at Hunstanton in August ('All you within the sound of my voice' was his favourite echo of those days!) and whilst an undergraduate he had kept up a close association with boys at The Perse by helping with the Crusader Bible Class. His conversational humour tended towards the 'tea and biscuits after the meeting' variety and in retrospect there seems to have been just a hint of the 'pale young curate' – then. (This is not quite the right phrase but it shall stand as even those who feel it might be misunderstood admit that it conveys the intention!) For the boys in his House or in the Sixth Form this was no handicap because there was so much sinewy spiritual strength below the surface. And so long as he was doing the job for which he was best suited it certainly was no handicap to him.

But it is one thing to run a house and teach English in an environment which for years has been one's natural habitat and it is quite another thing to pull up the roots geographically, to succeed a Headmaster of gigantic stature who over many years had forged a Common Room of rugged North Country worthies ('thou shalt have no other Gods but me!'), to dive in blindfold at the deep end – administratively speaking – and to come out buoyant and confident at the other end. It would have taken a tough experienced campaigner all his time to step into Costain's shoes and to have shown no wear and tear. And Donald was the pale young curate – then. There was nothing to take him out of the school – all his interest lay there. His Common Room, whilst friendly, were stubborn (which was not necessarily a fault) but after four years could still refer (in Donald's presence) to Costain as the 'Head' (which *was* a fault). He took little regular exercise, though he refereed some rugger, and his physical health clearly showed the lack of it. He sought no company, male or female, other than what was laid on by the daily round at School and was quite incapable of organizing a holiday except to go and address a conference or two. He began to doubt his capacity to cope. The symptoms are common enough, the remedy is simple – John Buchan outlined it in John McNab – but for most of us it consists of a 'to hell with it' and we escape to our other world. But Donald hadn't learned how to say 'to hell with it' – one

24

didn't talk like that over tea and biscuits and he had no other world. Someone, somewhere must have suggested it or unconsciously sown the seed for one day he was discovered hitting a golf ball – on the school playing fields – and from that moment onwards he grew upwards and outwards. God moves in a mysterious way.

(It should be said that one or two of those who have read this in preparation have suggested that too much importance was being attached to the golf angle. They may be right but the fact remains that round about the time when Donald started to play golf, he indubitably became a very different and a much tougher and more resilient person.)

A momentous decision. For a start he got regular exercise and it took him right out of the school. He became absorbed in the teasing pitfalls of the game and there can be little doubt that he got more real pleasure out of playing golf than out of any other non-intellectual pursuit. (May all golf writers and instructors take that remark with forbearance.) Later he became Golf Secretary of the Headmasters' Conference and was instrumental in causing it to meet at St Andrews! As ancillary benefits of the game, he played and met with a kindly people whom he had never previously known to exist and who themselves didn't know a Methodist from a bus driver. When he came back to school after his 18 holes at Conway where he normally played, he came back refreshed and tired, relaxed by the infinite release of this other world. His golfing friends in their way were, like him, unconscious evangelists.

He was bigly built, an experienced player of ball games, very determined and quite ungraceful. The result was that from time to time he hit the ball enormous distances and from time to time he sliced prodigiously. To what extent he was handicapped by the loss of his eye after he had been playing for some years it is hard to say but, to all people who start a game at 45 its movements don't come naturally and muscles and joints don't co-ordinate predictably enough to lay the foundations of a technique. He was given a handicap of twelve but he never returned a card. Two or three holes he might play like a single figure man but they would be followed by much more human figures. Twice he did a hole in one, the first time about a week after he had started playing on the old course at Upper Colwyn Bay and the second time at Conway in his last year. He was, of course, delighted when he was on form ('You've only to relax and keep your head down,' he would mutter), but one could never picture him really enjoying a regular 3 or 4 over par with all the human errors eliminated and only the professional ones left to conquer. His speed off the tee and round the course generally was at the double. He swept round and waited for no man: there was always the next shot to be played, the previous error to be redeemed or someone else's ball to be found in the gorse. He was far too impatient to linger looking for his own.

Chapter 4

When Donald Hughes was being interviewed by the Governors for the Headmastership of Rydal he was at pains to make it quite clear that if he were expected to control the finances of the school, or even to interest himself in them, then the Governors and he should part whilst they were still friends. He was no starry-eyed idealist, nor was he an absent-minded professor, but he would have found it difficult to mend a fuse: a boiled egg had an even chance of being under- or over-done. On the rare occasions on which he arbitrarily decided to 'wash' his car the result was a most extraordinary striped effect over the bodywork and a windscreen bleary with dirt. He once expounded the wonders of a magic wand that cleaned, polished and did the lot in a flash. 'No, Donald, it can't really do that!' 'I'll show you.' He went to fetch it and demonstrated on the newly decorated wall of the room, leaving a rich smear of oil. He parked his car in the Avenue outside School with a fine disregard for the line of the pavement (and it was generally necessary for his friends to point out when his tyres showed signs of wear). Paul, a friend of his aged 4, noticed this and met him on the steps of the school. 'Hello; you've parked your car very badly.' 'Have I?' (in some surprise). 'Come and show me.' Hand in hand they went. It was three feet out in front and five at the rear. The point was taken but the lesson not learned.

His remarkably quick reactions as a driver enabled him to overcome the handicap of having only one eye and he drove fast, albeit on his brakes, and with a sort of exuberance. 'That's what bumpers are for, isn't it?' he asked after some slight confusion at the entrance to the Mersey Tunnel. Towards other drivers on the road he was occasionally less than generous in his comments. 'You naughty man' he would exclaim and shake his fist as someone cut in exactly as he had done a moment earlier. But these were not eccentricities, simply indications that he accepted (gleefully) the fact that practical matters – providing one avoided embarrassing or inconveniencing others – were not his long suit and that it was better to concentrate on what he *could* do and leave others to make the world go round.

His wardrobe was surprising and seemed to be nearly the only example of extravagance in his life. Changing his car every two years he would defend as an economy which, with his mileage, was probably true. He specialized in Fords and was indignant when after buying a G.T. he found his insurance premium had risen. 'What does G.T. mean, anyhow?' He had an enormous number of suits, none of which made him appear really tidy: indeed he gave his tailor no chance for despite an impressive frame he never 'held' himself as a tailor hopes when he measures you and once he got into a chair he was all over the place and coat, waistcoat and trousers were rapidly reduced to rucked-up rags. For many years he smoked a pipe but round about 1963 when there was the first great drive about lung cancer he gave up smoking as an example to the School. Not long afterwards he resumed smoking but this time it was cigars, not on a Churchillian scale but quite frequently in the evenings. There is delightful inconsistency here because even from a medical point of view it seems that pipes and cigars are equally (un)harmful.

At one time at Rydal no games at all were allowed on Sundays except large numbers of unofficial cricket 'matches' of two or three a side. In the evenings twenty or thirty of these took place at once on one ground. But tennis was not allowed nor could boys go to watch Sunday cricket at Rhos, nor could they play golf. The cricket nets were out of bounds not because of the Commandments but to save the wickets! In later years the whole picture became even more splendidly uncertain and one never *quite* knew what was breaking the Sabbath and what was sanctified. Mass cricket in the evenings changed to unofficial but very serious soccer, the tennis courts became successively in bounds to prefects in the evenings and then to everyone in the afternoons, but watching cricket at Rhos was never openly approved and to be seen carrying golf clubs after morning service was emphatically a breach. Donald's attitude towards this vexed question was partly one of principle and partly a concern that the feelings of others – neighbours and parents – should not be hurt.

On tour with the Dolphins Cricket Club Sunday cricket was never played except on two occasions when the side played under the title of A. N. Other's XI. And during one holiday after Sunday lunch Donald and friend suddenly jumped into his car and drove 50 miles to Harlech where he wandered over the course – clubless – playing those dream shots which on weekdays never seemed to function. (To those who claimed that they 'Worshipped God in Nature' instead of going to church on Sunday morning he replied that it wasn't really the same as 'blaspheming in a bunker'.) He allowed sailing at Rydal on Sundays on the grounds that it didn't employ anyone else and that it was a very biblical activity. 'The only reason you object,' he said, 'is because the boys are enjoying themselves.' These and many other splendid foibles endeared him to those near and those not so near because it was possible to identify in them one's own characteristics; and taking into account the rest of his make-up that gave one hope – and good company!

His favourite drink was ginger-beer and lime, a mixture which he first of all persuaded the Dolphins was the Methodists' shandy and then even managed to popularize in the bar at the Grange C.C. in Edinburgh on tour: so much so that they ran out of one or both of the ingredients. But on a trip to Bavaria and Switzerland in 1966 he acceded to a suggestion and 'following the custom of the country' took wine at dinner. The first toast he proposed on the first night was to the office of Secretary of the Methodist Conference. A glass each night was the routine but he stopped this on the way home as soon as he stepped on the (British) ship at Rotterdam. Inquiries proved that this had nothing to do with an Insurance Policy.

At times the pressures of the golf course proved too great for his forbearance and at the Lancaster Golf Club on the way home from a fortnight's golf in Scotland where he had been gradually but inexorably reduced to his partner's form on eight different courses, he was joined by two irresponsible friends who, from about the third hole onwards, found themselves giggling, as sometimes people will for no real reason, though some unusual things did happen to the ball on (and only just off) the tee. Gradually Donald's game, already uncertain after the ordeal in Scotland, was torn to shreds and about halfway round the whole edifice of restraint collapsed and he threw his clubs into a handy ditch. The sort of thing was very good for him and most heartening for his friends – it helped so much to close the gap between his 'other level' and the one most of us live on. The golf part of the Scottish trip had included Dumfries, Gullane 1 and 2, Grantown-on-Spey, Strathpeffer, nine holes into a gale and horizontal wind at Dornoch, Newtonmore, Pitlochry and Rosemount where he came near to breaking a plate glass window in the clubhouse. The window faces on to the 18th green, separated from it by flagstones. Donald's last chip was through and bounced interestingly on the flagstones but regrettably missed the window. At Gullane two nights were spent at Greywalls, the gracious hotel which gives on to the course at Muirfield. 'Thou shalt not covet!' Donald hadn't bothered to get the necessary introductions for this holy of holies and so he could only gaze – from bedroom window, from dining-room, from lounge, on to the course. During one golf-free day he was persuaded to go to John O'Groats and for a few seconds between Wick and Thurso he unconcernedly drove at about 55 mph. on the grass verge instead of on the road. As far as he was concerned this was not even an occasion for comment and much less excuse or apology!

A Sunday jaunt took in morning service at Tongue and a sermon by Dr Erik Routley from the opening service of the Edinburgh Festival, listened to on the car radio on the shores of Loch Eribol. But on the whole unless there was golf, Scotland, for him, wasn't up to much, and his delight when a colleague on the Headmasters' Conference turned up at the same hotel in Gatehouse of Fleet was unfeigned.

As far as food was concerned he was a disappointing customer. At one time he had a passion for cream cakes – Matthews' (now pulled down) in Trinity Street was his favourite Cambridge coffee house – but apart from these cakes he practically never knew or cared what he was eating. He ate at an immense speed and if forced to make a choice from a menu would invariably say after a few moments' formal thought – 'I think I'll have an omelette.' Abroad he would unravel the immense German titles on the menu with the aid of a dictionary but this was an intellectual exercise rather than a gastronomic precaution. He also became a master (and revelled in it) at ordering early morning tea in German on the room telephone – 'Am apparat!' In fact he had a sort of vanity about his ability to make himself understood in French or German and there was much gesture accompanying his free use of idiom. He clearly had (latent) a gift for languages and the varying processes of thought in each language intrigued him. His stories involving broken English (German parachutists and the Home Guard, for instance) were given with a wealth of characterization which never varied, and he had one American accent for all occasions. He had been brought up on the direct method at The Perse by a bearded giant called De Glen. 'Je frappe Tidbury!' 'Que fais-je?' 'Vous frappez Tidbury.' Who was Tidbury and how often was he frapped? Donald would always quote this to illustrate De Glen's teaching.

He had a nice line in one or two eminent Methodists in the pulpit and at least one famous Old Leysian who spoke rather curiously was in his repertoire but throughout all these turns he remained Hughes imitating Hughes imitating X. This same Old Leysian who spoke out of only the right corner of his mouth – and that with frequency – congratulated Donald after an early sermon in the Leys Chapel but took him on one side and suggested that he spoke more clearly as he was very difficult to hear!

It is a fact that the Old Leysian had a point and Donald could be extremely conversational in some of his public utterances. Of course, he loathed anything savouring of rhetoric but even the sheer physical effort of speaking loud – or shouting – faintly repelled him and what began as a shout often ended up in an apologetic tone. In his days at

The Leys – during the exile in Scotland – he discovered that he owned a fairly impressive baritone voice and he did every justice to the part of the Mikado in the school production at Pitlochry. Indeed probably the loudest noise he ever made was the Mikado's maniacal laugh in the middle of his song. He sang on one occasion in public at Rydal – in the Dining Hall during a summer half-term 'floorshow' and dance. Ever mischievously eager to appear in some unusual role he delighted his audience with a completely meaningless pseudo-sophisticated revue song lifted from an operetta of his of earlier years.

We're William and Mary, we're demon and fairy,
We're John and we're James, we're pictures and frames,
Two halves of a ticket and cricket and wicket,
We're two of a kind!
We're cowboy and lasso, Matisse and Picasso,
We're Crosby and Hope, hot water and soap,
We're onions and leeks, we are Worrell and Weekes,
We're two of a kind!
You are all my past and all my future as well;
You are all the secrets I am trying to tell;
We're flocks and we're herds, we are music and words,
We're Aston and Villa, ice and vanilla,
We're skin and we're bone and we're Darby and Joan,
We're two of a kind!

But his greatest moment of premeditated folly occurred when he opened the new swimming-pool at Rydal on Speech Day by diving in fully clothed before a gathering of Governors, Parents, Boys, Dignitaries – the Lot. This caused the local paper to exclaim in bold type – 'Head First' – which earned them ten out of ten for succinctness.

In earlier days he had played many a surprising role in end of term shows at The Leys, ranging from broad farce to lurid melodrama. He wrote most of the shows, too, and he could turn out trivial rhyming couplets for pantomime or Sweeny Todd prose for 'The Threatened Homestead' with apparently no effort. His greatest roles were those of the Demon King in a burlesque pantomime, Miss Hannah Smurthwaite of St Prunella's College in a cricket skit on 'Ruddigore' and Harold Harfwit in 'The Threatened Homestead'. This latter had a distinguished supporting cast from The Leys Common Room.

He produced an historical drama entitled 'Macdeaf' – or 'Murder at Killicrankie' – which included the character of Young Seaweed and there were sundry sketches which he wrote about the Home Guard and local life at Pitlochry containing such deathless verse as 'I'm Home Harold, My shotgun's double-barrelled' or this pithy advertisement –

The visitors' prospects are rosy,
For the neighbourhood's homely and cosy;
All things that are nice
You can buy – at a price,
From the go-ahead Mr Pelosi

(An Italian 'business' man with a sweet, etc., shop in Pitlochry. This verse delighted the taciturn locals who 'liked it fine'.)

At some point, too, an end of term review of his included a domestic version of Jack Strachey's sophisticated classic entitled 'Leys Schoolish Things' –

Home guard manoeuvres after Sunday dinner;
And coming back to read with Conrad Skinner[1]
The Second Book of Kings –
Leys Schoolish Things, remind me of you.

In the Batsman's Bride, an opera about village cricket,[2] he skilfully and shamelessly burlesqued Gilbert, Shakespeare and BBC Commentators as well as including some 'original' lyrics. This, for instance, has a wistful charm:

---

[1] Rev. C. A. Skinner, then Chaplain of The Leys.
[2] See page 219.

When I was a little tiny boy,
(Dew on the wicket and shine on the ball);
My Father's pride, my Mother's joy,
Willow in the woods is the King of them all;
They all had hopes that I should be
A great, big shot at the top of the tree;
But nobody knew my secret dream
One day to be captain of the village team.

And The Umpire's Soliloquy – 'Lb or not Lb – that is the question' is a gem of craftsmanship. This work received several broadcast performances – and is still performed by amateur societies – but despite the fact that he kept up a steady bombardment of the BBC for a televised production it was never shown. He had written two earlier operettas, one at The Leys – a slightly self-conscious three-act semicomic affair with a 'message' about the Goddess of Peace and a Dictator – and a shorter one at Rydal – 'The Headmaster's Daughter'[1] in which he pilloried the Ministry of Education for a lunatic piece of legislation regarding the age at which O Level might first be taken.

This included one or two vintage verses which seemed almost to race away from the pen so slick were they:

Write promptly, politely
To Truman and Knightley
Success it will certainly bring;
And even a rabbit has
Prospects with Gabbitas,
Gabbitas aided by Thring.
For agents scholastic
Are iconoclastic . . .

There were also three scintillating songs which decorated Rydalian concerts: the first[2] poked genial fun at the 'Abersoch set':

---

[1] See page 233.
[2] See page 213.

34

The people in Society who really count the most
Have hitched the boat behind the Jag and are heading for the coast

the second,[1] written for the installation reception of the Mayor of
Colwyn Bay, extolled in fulsome and laughable verse the varied
attractions of Colwyn Bay in particular and North Wales in general:

I dream of Myfanwy, the belle of Deganwy
  For ever the Queen of my heart;
(Or was it Anharrog, the doll from
    Dolgarrog?
I never could tell them apart!)

And the third did a similar job for East Yorkshire and a talented
Rydalian family on the occasion of a concert in aid of a village
Methodist chapel. Although these were 'occasional pieces' they are so
exuberant that their topical references transcend the boundaries of
time and space and they remain a joy to read.

After leaving The Leys where he had frequently produced
Shakespeare with great distinction as well as the more frivolous enter-
tainments he found few opportunities for involvement in drama at
Rydal. He wrote one three-act play for a winter term production and a
one-act drama for a House Competition, but undoubtedly his finest
hour was his production of *King Lear* in 1965. He took immense pains
over this and enlisted the skills and support of every strata of school
society. During his Bavarian holiday, already referred to, whilst his
travelling companion spent the evenings in slothful contemplation on
a balcony sofa, he was hard at it with text and notebook and though
his immense preparation and hours of producing completely exhausted
him he had the satisfaction of knowing that he mounted as fine a school
Shakespearean performance as his audience were ever likely to see.

His papers reveal a number of other plays and stories and at the
time of his death he was actually engaged in writing a thriller. These

---

[1] See page 216.

were all as full of ideas as they were empty of characters: he was interested in the people only in so far as they were useful for uttering his arguments and they seldom had any depth of character or personality. As like as not they would be called John Smith: anything more dimensional than that might interest his readers in them as people and that would obstruct their view of the 'argument'. In this as in other aspects of his art he had something in common with W. S. Gilbert (who, for instance, could write a character sketch of Nanki Pooh?) though this did not include anything like a malevolence towards the Katishas of this world. The intelligent clarity which always marked Donald's writing was a clear gift from his father, as was his humour. This ranged from the erudite and scholarly to real knockabout and is evident (at least the latter is) whenever two or three Hughes are gathered together. He was not only a story teller with a story for every occasion – or perhaps an occasion for every story – but a master of repartee. When he was visiting a Housemaster one evening the son – teaching temporarily at a prep school – rang up. His mother returned after answering the phone and said 'That was Frankie: he's wanting his Bible and his swimming trunks.' 'Why, is he becoming a Baptist?' asked Donald. As he passed a parrot in a house in Bala the bird suddenly said 'I beg your pardon': without pause for breath in his conversation Donald murmured 'think nothing of it'. He himself told the story of a friend of his uncle who (according to Donald) was reported to have said 'Well, having a gift for repartee, I told him to go to hell!'

Much of his facility with words and rhyme and argument is evident in the large amount of more serious verse, story and parable which is dealt with elsewhere. Just as he might deliver a lecture on Christianity and Humanism in the afternoon to a Conference and in the evening move the cricket dinner to gales of laughter, so he could with one hand dash off nonsense rhymes about a hot water bottle[1] and with the other compose a deeply devotional hymn.[2] A man for all seasons.

---

[1] See page 215.
[2] See pages 207, 208.

Chapter 5

A Leysian, writing about Donald Hughes suggested that the decision to leave The Leys and become a Headmaster was a most difficult one for him because he must have known that the change would inevitably weaken the intimate associations with the boys which he so treasured. Exactly what Donald knew or feared we don't know, though it is hardly likely that he ever envisaged operating as Headmaster from some Olympian platform and it is doubtful if anything particular ever occurred to him about the details of the job. Things have a way of sorting themselves out according to how one sees the job, and once having disposed of the business side of the school – and how glad the Governors must have been that he didn't pretend! – he was prepared to take things as they came. But, of course, one selects and if there are certain things one does very well one tends to steer the work in that direction. He did more than steer it – he bent it. As a result, whilst being a Headmaster he operated on Housemaster level so to speak, certainly as far as the boys were concerned, and his inability to stop being a Housemaster was more than anything else the most powerful source of his influence over them. There was no conscious abdication of the office of Headmaster: those things which had to be done by a Headmaster he did because 'someone had to do it': as soon as the inescapable chores were done he, as it were, took off his gown and became himself again.

This was evident not only in public relations within the school but also in matters of teaching. He never taught less than 15 periods a week throughout his time at Rydal and if he were away and missed periods he would make them up immediately on return. This was partly conscientousness and partly because he liked teaching; he liked the give and take of discussion and resented anything that interrupted it! Why then did he forsake the green pastures of Housemastering and teaching for the exposed peaks of Headmastering? Did he ever regret it? It is fairly certain that he never regretted it for it brought him into touch with problems and people which, whatever the anxieties and responsibilities of the job, were endlessly fascinating and absorbing. And do we have to have a reason for his wanting to become a Headmaster? Is it unreasonable that he should have had that much ambition? (The picture won't tarnish.) The Leys had already had one Mr Chips and he was not wanting to be a second. There *could* have been a call but more likely he saw it as a chance to develop the whole art of schoolmastering in all its dimensions.

At The Leys he will be remembered as a quite extraordinary Housemaster (no gimmicks or stunts), for all the things that one imagined a good Housemaster to be he was: it actually worked! As a teacher of English, too, he had few peers and in drama, debate and discussion he was the ideal inspiration and foil for the jaunty assertions of youth. The Essay Club – a paper and discussion group which he ran – was possibly the medium which gave him the best opportunities of intellectual close combat. But because he was so brilliant at that level he unconsciously muzzled a number of less extrovert members – they literally couldn't get a word in and after a time it became necessary to start a Junior Essay Club with a colleague in the Chair. The chairman was chosen for his ability to maintain silence (his own) and in this way ensure that the members were all gradually able to sharpen their conversational claws on each other before they graduated to the Senior Essay Club where it was necessary to attack on the slightest pause in the Chairman's argument. This inability to keep quiet 'in company' became fairly noticeable in later years at Rydal: he would tend to monopolize the conversation (and who better?) sometimes as if he felt it was expected of him and, at others, out of sheer habit. And he could become rather obviously restless if the topic under discussion was something in which he had no interest. Tom Green, his headmaster friend already mentioned, once when staying with Donald spent twenty minutes talking about the scenery of Wester Ross with a fellow enthusiast. Donald visibly and almost audibly itched! As likely as not he would put up with this sort of situation for a few minutes and then blow the whole thing sky-high with some facetious comment which was easily used as his own conversational launching pad. He was a superb talker and if one calls him only a moderate listener it must be understood that when it really mattered he could yield the floor. Anything less like a bore it would be hard to imagine – and even that suggests a completely false picture.

Governors, parents, Old Boys, colleagues and boys: these were the people he mainly dealt with and it is hard to say who came off best, since he was the same person to all of them. Governors of a school – to anyone who works in the school – are a somewhat remote entity and only those who regularly attend their meetings can properly understand the relationship between a Governing Body and a Headmaster. As far as Donald Hughes was concerned they were simply a collection of friends whom he met sometimes at Crewe and sometimes at Rydal in order to discuss problems affecting the school. He knew and liked them and expressed his opinion on educational topics and policy regarding the school but it hardly occurred to him or them that he was their employee. The concept was almost vulgar.

To parents he must have been like a friendly inn-keeper at the end of a long, stormy journey. From the moment when he showed prospective parents round the school ('I have a customer') till the day on which their boy left the school – and after – those parents must have been sure of one thing at least in life: their son and they need never again wonder where to turn for advice. In this context he can have had no superiors anywhere.

It is now an open secret that for many years he made financial provision from his own pocket to enable certain boys to continue and complete their school careers when otherwise they would have had to leave. This personal scholarship fund naturally was administered quite anonymously but one of the objects of the Donald Hughes Memorial Fund is to continue the work which he had begun in this field and which is not touched by the provisions of ordinary scholarship awards.

A few years before his death he apologetically suggested that after the Summer Half-term Concert a few parents might be interested if he briefly spoke about a few of the problems of authority and discipline which schoolmasters and parents had in common in a permissive age. It was expected that 40 to 50 might come into the Dining Hall to hear him. In the event so many turned up that he had to address the packed assembly standing on a table – this was at 10.0 p.m. during a social weekend in summer! He was quite unnerved by the response and the fact that so many bewildered parents had put so much trust in him.

There might have been moments when their trust would have temporarily wavered had they but known that even if he seldom forgot a face he could forget a name – particularly the Christian name of a boy. 'And how do you think Michael is getting on?' asked a beaming mother. 'Well, what's your reaction?' Donald would say, treading water. Question and counter-question would continue for some time until the surname finally dropped. Home and dry, he thought, only to discover that the mother had married a second time and changed her name! He once had a father in his study who wanted to see his son urgently – 'May I see Timothy?' 'Certainly' – playing for time. By infinite guile he elicited that the boy was in Va and, despairing of finding the surname he went to Va, asked anyone called Timothy to stand up and out of three who stood up he chose the one who most resembled the waiting father. He was dead on target.

Only those who had contacts at Rydal before Donald Hughes became Headmaster can possibly appreciate the extent of the influence of the Rev. A. J. Costain amongst the Old Rydalians of that time. A Scottish chieftain would have been proud to command half such allegiance. Behind the almost mystical reverence in which he was held was a blustering, bantering, rough and tumble and indestructible edifice. How would the Tribe accept his successor – externally so completely different? (It is one of life's endless fascinations that the externals can be so completely misleading. A.J.C. and D.W.H. were really exactly the same in their ultimate aims.) In the event the Old Rydalians had no choice: they simply succumbed to his quality. True, he made enormous efforts from the start to show them that as far as he was concerned they were as much a part of the school as anyone else: the fact that he had a very real admiration for A.J.C. was no handicap and that, in his way, he was as good an after-dinner speaker as the Old Man himself put him well on the road to acceptance. After that it was simply a matter of the grape-vine doing its stuff and Donald being himself. They had no choice.

His policy towards Old Rydalians may be illustrated – up to a point – by a remark he made at a Governors' Meeting when he explained that he believed that the sons of Old Rydalians should be admitted to Rydal even if they were not up to the normal required academic standard. A short time after, a son of a Governor (himself a boy at school) who had heard this statement of policy from his father, was sitting near Donald at school lunch and the conversation centred around monkeys, apes and gorillas and how much they could be taught. Donald, whilst admitting that they could be trained in a limited way suggested that a gorilla couldn't really expect to pass into Rydal, to which the boy retorted: 'Unless he happened to be the son of an Old Rydalian.'

Curiously enough it was probably in relations with the Common Room that Donald Hughes more nearly came unstuck than in any other direction. One fancies that the present old-timers viewing the whole span might suggest that there was never a difficulty or misunderstanding, but it would be a pity to ignore the intriguing paradox of a Common Room often infuriated by decisions lacking detail and inadequately communicated, and individual members who seldom if ever failed to react to the unself-conscious charm, consideration and apologies of their Headmaster when his 'errors' were pointed out. It took him much longer to gain acceptance by the Old Guard in the Common Room than by the Old Rydalians. There was a gap in age which, oddly enough, seemed harder to bridge than it does today. He was taking command in a post-second-war age of men who had taught and fought in the first World War. They had, under A.J.C., re-created Rydal and there was a rather tight parochialism about the place. The 'off-comer' remained an off-comer for four to five years while the ghost of A.J.C. gradually receded. And how impeccable was the behaviour of A.J.C. and Mrs Costain during this time: they retired to Abersoch from where they could have been, in the nicest way possible, a blooming nuisance. At no time did they attempt to 'come back' and their graciousness and understanding in retirement were a model.

As Donald became more secure and certain of himself so did his scope for error increase! To many men of brilliant minds the practicability and details of a scheme or reform are things seemingly put there specially to thwart progress. At times matters were left so much in the air at Masters' Meetings that it was impossible to tell whether they had ever happened or whether anything was ever decided. Meetings were held at the beginning and end of term and, if absolutely unavoidable, there might be an odd extra one thrown in. Minutes of the last meeting were read like some fairy story from long ago: subcommittees which were to report on board dusters or coat pegs dissolved without ever meeting. Suggestions that such vagueness was deliberate – a sort of calculated foible – appear to contradict not only his reluctance to scheme but the sometimes much more patent reason that he probably wanted to be on the 1st tee, and that he knew others had similar pressing engagements. This is not frivolous; he felt that nothing was gained by prolonging meetings and that their best justification was the opportunities they gave for the talkers to talk. Decisions could be taken much more rapidly and easily at other times.

And in the long run it didn't honestly matter because everyone recognized where the weaknesses lay and, out of loyalty, affection and sense of duty, remedied them. But there was wear and tear of the nerves: a boy would frequently be given leave to go away for some special (or not so special) reason and the housemaster would not be informed; he made a ruling that school prefects might go in the swimming bath at 10.0 p.m. and it did not become known to housemasters until the boys breezed into their houses at 10.30 p.m. plus. Of course, the bothers all blew over and in restrospect they seem petty enough – righteous indignation was maddeningly quick to deflate in his presence – but such instances in a boarding-school are twice daily and with events and people so closely overlapping, lack of orderly communication is the quickest way to give your colleagues ulcers. In this he excelled. But if a boy were in real trouble or difficulty the contact with the housemaster was total.

And whoever had a row with him? Whoever felt that the obviously professional end-product was not worth the apparently amateur means he used to achieve it? Where efficiency is the main slogan it can oust all sorts of worthwhile aspects of human nature which, whilst possibly redundant in the rat race, are meat and drink to a close community. Not that there was any conscious policy behind his method or lack of it; scheming, organization, de-centralization were time-consuming things which, since his mind was concentrated elsewhere, were quite easily ignored. And his colleagues, like the Old Rydalians, recognizing class when they saw it – and it always came peeping through – did their jobs without his supervision. He never looked over anyone's shoulder and no Common Room ever worked with less of an autocrat. A moan here, a bellyache there – the essential safety valves of men working under pressure and never mistaken by them or anyone else for anything but the inarticulate mumblings of admiration and affection which he inspired and received. There were, no doubt, a number of more academically high-powered Common Rooms around but in terms of co-operation and united aims there can have been few better in the business than that at Rydal.

His ability not to interfere – and even to sit back and enjoy his colleagues grappling with a situation which might soon become his – is well illustrated by the occasion when he was spending the evening as the guest of a housemaster. At 10.0 p.m. the Head of the House came to inform the housemaster that three boys were missing. A routine check of the house was made and the boys obviously *were* missing. At this point the Headmaster might well have risen and taken command. Not on your life! Donald lolled in his chair savouring the delights of his friend's discomfiture and being amply rewarded when the three boys

43

were discovered hiding in a cupboard, because there had been a collection for OXFAM in the house!

To the two official ladies in his life – Sally Jones, his housekeeper, and Hester Norris, his secretary – he was a source of perpetual joy, wonder and worry. In the style of G.K. Chesterton he was quite capable of wiring 'Am in Runcorn: where should I be?' These two ladies grew philosophical in his service; clairvoyant, too, since his engagement diary never told the whole truth and nothing but the truth. He might or might not remember to tell anyone that he was away, that there were guests for the weekend. If pressed for information about the coming week or so by those who had to minister to him he would assume an air of gruffness which at times barely concealed his view that 'women will worry so much'. He had no conception as to what went on behind the scenes and not a few of the problems which beset a kindly and easily-exploited man were marvellously eased for him by these two ladies who guarded and guided his business and social life. When he was properly tuned in he was consideration itself, but his un-methodical manner in the study probably cut both ways. It certainly meant less volume of work since things like typewritten memos, directions to Tom, Dick or Harry, etc., weren't his line of country. But his own handwriting was a nightmare and transcribing it made up in time for the absence of routine work which with a tycoon would certainly have occurred. (One of three crazes he succumbed to at various times was a 'method' of script for bad writers and when he tried he could be very legible. He also toyed with the learning of Welsh and paraded his grasp of idiom at St David's Day dinners. Most surprisingly of all, round about 1950, he subscribed to a course of instant piano playing called 'Klaverscribo' or some such name: he never got off the ground!) The drawers of his desk were stuffed with old cheque-books, insurance certificates, old University diaries, etc., etc. After his death it was necessary to sort out these drawers and it is little exaggeration to say that the right-hand drawer overflowed with cheque stubbs, insurance documents, etc., up to 1959 and the left-hand drawer from 1959 to 1967. He would have needed a new desk in 1968.

Of course these people with senses of humour like himself, Sally

Jones and Hester Norris, were hardly likely to fail to find common ground in any problem however irreconcilable, and chuckles, guffaws and – in one case certainly – helpless mirth were constant companions of this astonishing trio. One summer half term just before the parents' interviews were about to start, he decided to move a large rose bowl off his table. Hester Norris saw it was full and took it slowly and carefully – dribbling a little water – but he was not to be cheated, and, as impetuous as on the golf course, he seized the bowl and water positively cascaded all over the filing cabinets and floor. 'Laughter,' as they say. Enter the first parent. Exit Miss Norris with bucket and cloth.

A special Memorial issue of the Old Rydalian which was printed four months after his death was heavy with the sweet scent of Tribute. At the time it seemed right that those who had known and worked with him in different capacities should try briefly to assemble their thoughts. But there was one notable omission from the contributors – a boy. Old Boys featured – a senior prefect, a head of his house at The Leys, but they were writing from hindsight, years after the event. But the boy actually at school – what did he think then? How did Donald Hughes appear to him who knew nothing of other Headmasters?

Clearly he was first and foremost a very kind person, a gentle-man. He talked a great deal and most of the time anyone could understand what he said. He appeared to have a funny story – not just a grown-ups funny but a real funny – for every topic which came up and laughter was seldom missing from an English period, a sermon, lunch at High Table, the golf course, the bridge table or even a Games Committee. He looked the sort of person you could go to for advice for he never appeared to know *all* the answers: this made him accessible, not just geographically but as a fellow human being. He seemed to be interested in an amazing number of things and he was just as likely to be found at some lowly rugger division game as at an inter-school match. (Unable to attend a Liverpool performance of the Concert Choir – he was speaking at a Rotary Charter Night – he journeyed to the Wirral in order to hear the rehearsal.) He was passionately interested in the building programme of the School, particularly in the Memorial Hall (which he would visit nightly as it gradually rose from the ground) and the

Swimming Pool (which he visited pretty frequently after its completion).

The rebel who mistook his slack rein for permissiveness and challenged his quiet authority was of all boys the one likely to come nearest to his wide compassion. 'There, but for the grace of God,' he seemed to be saying and, together, Headmaster and rebel would set out on the long road to sanity. He assumed good sense and the wish to co-operate and the result was glad co-operation in 99 per cent of boys.

As a teacher he stimulated – and was not free from pedantry – causing the clever to think for themselves and the less gifted to find an interest where they suspected none existed. As a preacher he held his captive audience by early on establishing common ground, using words and experience which they understood, keeping a shrewd eye on the clock and never trying to preach more than one sermon at a time. He had firm views about compulsory chapel though when compulsory week-day evening prayers were abolished he was surprised to find himself having to argue for voluntary attendance against some of the Common Room, though his opponents were probably motivated less by spiritual reasons than by the feeling that the boys were getting away with something.

On his death the Methodist Recorder headed his obituary 'Donald Hughes – A Great Headmaster'. Exactly what we mean by great is getting harder to say every day but in stumbling towards a definition it is no good pointing to this or that virtue or talent. Greatness is an amalgam of many virtues plus a sort of relish which allows one to savour them all at once. And to pretend that greatness admits of no weak spot is to be uncritically blind and thus debase the currency. Who would deny Churchill greatness? And who would deny that he was irascible and at times unreasonable? We like our great men to be human for otherwise we cannot identify ourselves with them, and if human, then subject to human frailty. Granted that condition, a confident affirmation can be given to the Recorder's headline 'Donald Hughes – A Great Headmaster'.

Chapter 6

Memorial Services

Donald Hughes died on Saturday August 12th, 1967, during the summer holidays, and the funeral service was attended by the family and a few representatives of the Governors, Old Rydalians, the Common Room and friends. It was decided that there should be two Memorial Services at the beginning of the Autumn Term, the first for the School in the familiar surroundings of the Memorial Hall where an intimate and domestic atmosphere might prevail. The address at this service was given by the Rev. A. W. Hopkins, Chaplain of The Leys. The second service, for a more general congregation, was held in St John's Church, Colwyn Bay. Over eleven hundred people attended this public service and it was necessary to relay it to an overflow congregation in the Memorial Hall. The service was taken by the Rev. Dr E. Gordon Rupp, Principal of Wesley House, Cambridge, and the address was given by the Rev. K. Underwood, a former Chaplain of Rydal.

In addition to members of Donald Hughes' family and the Governors and Staff of both the Senior and Preparatory Schools there was a vast assembly of Old Rydalians. Many parents of past and present boys, members of the Rydal Association, local friends and neighbours and Old Leysians attended. Anglican, Nonconformist and Roman Catholic clergy, civic dignitaries of the Borough and Justices of the Peace and a large representation of Headmasters, from both H.M.C. and other schools, were also present. Societies and organizations represented included the North Wales Cricket Association, the Colwyn

Bay Cricket Club, the North Wales Rugby Football Union, the Colwyn Bay Rugby Football Club, the Rotary Clubs of Colwyn Bay and Conway, the Caernarvonshire Golf Club, the Old Penrhosian Association and the Rydal Youth Centre.

A man for all seasons.

Introduction to the selected writings

The selected works which follow are, with one or two exceptions, published for the first time. Grateful acknowledgment is made for permission to reprint those which already have been published. The decision to include in this selection nothing from the longer published works was taken because it seemed inadvisable to lift passages from their original contexts and impracticable to reprint the complete works. A list of these works can be found in an appendix.

Contrary to first fears a considerable amount of material was available from which the following selection was made. It covers a wide field and one can only hope that it presents an adequate picture of a writer and speaker whose reason and imagination (to use his own title) was complementary to a professional technique which enabled him effortlessly to tune in on any wavelength without the slightest lowering of standards. Some of his light verse is as superbly 'bad' and inventive as his papers and sermons are penetrating and wise. Words were used because they meant something and not because they sounded impressive, and he was never at a loss for a rhyme when the subject was frivolous.

Sermons and speeches sometimes suffer cruelly when read but in this case it seems that little has been lost. They make easy and compelling reading and because they so patently display the faith, humility and humour of the author they create for the stranger (and re-create for others) the personality behind the words and there can be no better reason for offering them. As to the choice there may be many opinions but there must be one responsibility. It was a question of what to leave out; how to strike a balance between the sermons on 'general topics' and those for special occasions and, in the book as a whole, to avoid overweighting it with sermons; for the manuscripts of speeches and occasional papers were much less numerous.

A critical analysis of the style and content of these utterances seems to be of no value at all. The style is so direct and the simplicity and skill of presentation so obvious that to elaborate on it would be to create a mystique or a cult. And the content? The Christian Message in the round, presented without a rant or a flamboyant gesture, making an equal appeal to the sophisticate and to the 'ordinary man'. It is a fact that the matter of his sermons changed little from his last years at The Leys to his last years at Rydal. But the manner of delivery and thus the impact of what he said matured enormously. He never spoke (technically) well but he learned to time what he said so that the point was made and he stood and 'moved' well in the pulpit.

A number of 'Experiments in Chapel' which were introduced in School services have been included. These were early experiments and, given time, he undoubtedly would have explored and developed a rich vein in this field.

Only two of his hymns have been included – in the Verse section. 'At a Farewell' has very special associations for many Rydalians and 'Penitence' is here printed in its original version and not in the truncated form in which it appears in a recent supplement. It is very much an expression of his faith. In a remarkable paper to the Hymn Society (see page 153) he approaches the problem of words with some diffidence and certainly his own words blaze no new trails nor is there any attempt to strike out a new style.

'The Truth about Cricket' is the only example which could be traced in manuscript form of his after-dinner speeches. There is a tape of another Cricket Speech but with slight local variations it is very much the same. Of his many speeches at Old Boys' Dinners and Rotary Charter Nights, etc., there is no trace. Most of them were off the cuff or at least off the envelope and in a way it is probably better that they should be allowed to linger only in affectionate memory. They were after all 'occasional', set in a mellow old-chap context and as such they were perfect. Let them remain so.

The light verse and extracts from the 'shows' are offered entirely without apology. They demonstrate as vividly as his sermons (and better in their way than his hymns) a facet of the portrait which the volume tries to present and if any reader finds them frivolous he is quite right. But 'not always on the mount may we . . .'! The attraction of his personality was that he found time for the frivolous and was very good at it and as has already been mentioned his 'bad' verse was superb. To exclude this section would be to shut away some of the happiest memories and by omission to distort the image.

Sermons

A SERMON FOR CHRISTMAS

I do not propose to interrupt this service with a long address. There is a sense in which the historic lessons and the familiar carols carry their own message and he would be very dull of soul who failed to hear it. But we must all be conscious of the dangers of familiarity. Year after year at this time we give ourselves up for a few days to the beloved ritual; we sing and read about a view of life from which the values of the world in which we live seem to grow increasingly remote; and when the interlude is over we return to the everyday world, in which there is no peace on earth and very little goodwill among men. Does it make any significant difference that 2,000 years ago the wise men were led by the star and the shepherds were called by the angels to that commonplace stable by an inn? We do well, I think, to pause for a moment and face squarely the question about Christmas which has to be asked and answered: is this fact or fiction? Is it the loveliest fairy-tale that men have ever invented, or is it the highest truth about God and man that has ever been granted to the human race?

The carol with which our service opens begins and ends like a fairy-tale: perhaps that is why, in the Methodist hymn-book it appears in the section 'For little children'. 'Once upon a time' is the traditional opening, and we are reminded of it as we sing 'Once in royal David's city stood a lowly cattle shed'. And as we finish the fairy-tale with the time-honoured ending – 'They all lived happily ever after', so we sing 'And our eyes at last shall see Him through His own redeeming love'.

It is easy for the cynic to see in this nothing more than another example of man's pathetic wishful thinking, and to find no help here for the race in its tragic predicament.

But the keywords of the carol are those of the tremendous statement with which the second verse opens:

He came down to earth from heaven
Who is God and Lord of all

That is the belief which we share as Christians and if we really believe it there is no limit to its revolutionary power in our lives and in the life of the world.

It means first of all that we are quite wrong in our worship of power. When God revealed Himself as a man He came, not to imperial Rome, but to subject Palestine; not to a family of influence and prestige but to a working peasant; not to a royal palace, but to a stable because there was no room for Him in the inn. And the only people who recognized the significance of this unique event were those who were qualified to recognize it by their own humility: the little group round the manger contained no clever people. It consisted of wise men who were humble enough to follow where their wisdom led and uneducated shepherds whose ears were open to the heavenly song. If we are to prove for ourselves that Christmas is fact and not fiction we must start there and accept God's gift in humility. We must give up the idea, to which our age is so prone, that given time we can save ourselves with a little more knowledge and a little more power.

The second message for us, in this great historic fact in which our religion is rooted, is that God always reveals Himself in the simple, ordinary things of life; it is there that we must find Him and in that context that we must serve Him. We talk as if the great problems of life were at the top and must be solved by important people at that level. We are always saying that they ought to do something about it and when we say 'They' we mean Prime Ministers and Foreign Secretaries and Archbishops. But the problems which vex the world are rooted in the everyday sins and faults of ordinary people like ourselves: that is why God revealed Himself at a level at which we all can understand

Him. His challenge is not to empires and leaders but to wise men and shepherds – that is to the learned and to the ignorant, to the privileged and the unprivileged, to all men and to every man. There is no magic let loose in the world at Christmas which will miraculously refute Communism, baffle the Kremlin and drive the Chinese back over the Korean border; but God's gift is offered to you and to me and if we will accept it then some more of His power may be released into the world through our lives.

And lastly, Christmas brings to us the assurance that God is Love. This means that the ultimate nature of life is good and not bad: that love, and kindliness, compassion and mercy are the realities, and that what we call the grim realities of life – hatred, oppression, cruelty and war – are illusions in the hell which man has made of God's world. That is an assurance of which we stand in very great need today. If we look out on to the world without it we shall find much ground for despondency and despair, and for the belief that the world has been given over into the hands of the powers of evil. But because of the message of Christmas we know that evil has no lasting power: in the affairs of the world, and in our own individual affairs, the last word will be spoken, not by those who have power over legions of men and destructive techniques, but by God, and we know that He is love, because only love gives freely, and He has given His only son, that whosoever believeth in Him should not perish.

Let us then adore Him and let us offer to Him our lives in return for the life that He gave for us: so shall we prove, for ourselves and to others, that this Christian festival which we keep is no empty ritual, but the love and the saving power of God, released into the world to bring peace on earth and goodwill amongst men.

A SERMON FOR THE NEW YEAR

*'Now therefore make a new cart and take the ark of the Lord and lay
it upon the cart'*

I Samuel VI, 7–8

At the beginning of a new year we all tend to attach a great deal of importance to novelty, and I suppose that this is especially true at the beginning of a new decade. These milestones of the calendar are quite artificial, of course: nothing really new comes into being because we now see 1960 at the top of our papers, where formerly we saw 1959, and because we now talk about living in the Sixties, whereas we used to live, as we say, in the Fifties. But in the realm of ideas things are what we think them to be, and there is no doubt that the contemporary accent is on the new. We have only just stopped wishing each other a Happy New Year: that we go on doing this every twelve months, without any startling differences happening, might seem to a cynic a triumph of hope over experience, but the human animal is incurably optimistic and the old formula comes very easily to the tongue.

There is no denying that newness has a glamour all of its own. Very early in life children are excited by the strange and glossy look of toys and presents that are new. Later on, everyone knows what loving care he lavishes on a new bicycle, with one or two refinements that the old one didn't possess, or a new cricket bat or tennis racquet which, we believe, will somehow play the strokes that we haven't managed to play with the old one. It is a tremendous moment, at any stage of your life, when you move into the new house, or the new car stands outside the door. One of the exciting things about the age in which we live is

58

the astonishing variety of new things with which we are continually being confronted. If you were asked to write an essay on the year 1970 most of you would probably spend most of your time describing the things which will be commonplace then and which we do not now possess – colour television showing continuously in every room in the house, and helicopters and hovercraft so that we may have traffic jams in three dimensions and that sort of thing.

It sometimes seems that what really erects barriers between the generations is this question of newness. To the young it often appears that their elders, at some stage in their development, become so attached to the things that they knew that they are rendered incapable of appreciating anything else. Many of you are by now tired of being told how much better everything was a generation ago – before the war, or when I was your age, my boy, or in the good old days. Wherever you look, in politics, or the arts or in games or in clothing you meet the same old story. And yet, oddly enough, nobody claims that medical science, for example, or physics, were more advanced twenty-five years ago, or that aeroplanes and cars, or even men, could move as fast then as now. So you tend to assume that your elders are funny that way and that they can't help it and you extend to them a kindly indulgence, knowing that they are in the wrong and quite unaware that you will make similar demands on the charity of the next generation.

It is obviously quite wrong to stop appreciating new things at a certain age and value only the things that you happen to know already. I suppose that we go on being educated as long as we are capable of enjoying and evaluating new experiences and that when we can no longer do that we are no longer fully alive. It may be that it is a phase that people go through: you may have observed that the old are often more tolerant than the middle-aged. But, having said that, I want also to say that there is nothing more half-baked than the assumption that anything new must be better than anything old. If your education doesn't deliver you from that belief then, you may know a lot, but you aren't properly educated at all. Only in some things is novelty an advantage: a shirt? – yes. But a dentist? A pilot?

59

The point is that no-one can find out the whole of truth in a life-time. Unless we are prepared to take a certain amount on trust from those who have gone before us there can never be such a thing as pro-gress. We have a proverb that the burnt child dreads the fire, but every child doesn't have to go through this experience: children who have heard about the burnt child dread the fire too. In every department of life the principle holds good that experience and experiment need one another. If you have only experience you soon suffer decay and atrophy: if you have only experiment you soon get lost in chaos and anarchy.

It is easy enough to test the value of old things. Those which have stood the test of time, as we say, and proved their value in succeeding generations are entitled to be regarded with especial respect: only an idiot thinks, for example, that Shakespeare and Michelangelo and Bach are still on trial. The test of new things is not so easy, but we can say at least that valuable new things are likely to be in some way an extension of the old, since the basic things about human life don't really change very much. It may take a good deal of patient study before we discover that contemporary movements in literature and art or in music and architecture which appear to be revolutionary are really evolutionary, but if those who are qualified to do so tell us that that is what the new thing with which we are concerned really is, then that is the kind of change that we may welcome.

You couldn't have a better example of what a school ought to be. We are what we are because of our past: This is our 75th year and you do well to look back on our tradition with pride. But if you were still the same as you were in 1870, or twenty-five years ago or even ten, then you would have little to be proud about. It is for you (and me) to maintain and foster the appropriate contribution that 1960 has to make.

You may wonder what this has to do with religion and why I choose to talk about it in a period which is usually devoted to a sermon. Here is the reason. You and I can't begin to understand what Christianity is about until we realize that it is all the time concerned with the old and the new. That is the point of the text. The ark of the Lord represented the old tradition of the faith: they put the old ark on a new cart. Jesus said that he came, not to destroy the law but to fulfil it: He also said that He came to give men life and to give it abundantly. Behold I make all things new: Jesus Christ, the same yesterday, today and forever. There is no more tragic misunderstanding than the illusion that young people suffer from very often: that is, that religion is the concern of the old. I want to remind you of one or two things.

Our Lord was a young man throughout his ministry and He was still a young man when they crucified Him. People thought many things about Him, but no-one ever thought Him stuffy or respectable. If He appeared among us today with the same teaching it would still strike people as new. What would we think of a man who told us to treat our enemies and our friends in exactly the same way: how many of us agree with that? That we ought never to resent an injury: if a man take your coat... that the true measure of success was the number of people whom we could serve: is that your idea of success? Who told very bad people that they were forgiven when they did no more than say that they were sorry, and very good people that they could not be forgiven because they were unforgiving? We are still arguing about whether we ought to hang criminals or not. There is a strange sort of idea that we are all Christians now: the fact is that there is nothing in Communism, or in the wild revolts of the angry young men, which is nearly as foreign to the accepted standards of respectable society as the Sermon on the Mount. If it is true, as has been said, that Jesus was crucified for being ahead of his time then He would be very likely to meet with a similar fate today.

The Christian faith is 2,000 years old, but if we are really to practise it in the Sixties we shall all have to embark on something new. There is nothing that can come to us in the changing world in which we live that can make it absolute or irrelevant. For it is not simply an immutable set of beliefs: it is a way of life, and its law is the law of life – growth and development. Just as you and I are physically changing all the time and yet remaining the same people, so we need a faith and a way which is always changing and yet always remains the same thing. Where do you expect to find it? This is what the doctrine of the Holy Spirit is about.

I am the way, the Truth and the Life. I am Alpha and Omega, the beginning and the end. Jesus Christ, the same yesterday, today and forever.

A SERMON FOR EASTER

Everybody knows that the word 'gospel' means 'good news', but everyone doesn't know how good is the news of the gospel. The trouble about good news, as we experience it, is that it is so partial and impermanent. I remember during the dark days of the war how we all looked forward to the remote time when the news would begin to be good. And at last the time came, with the news first of the collapse of Italian resistance, later of victory in Europe, and finally of victory in the Far East as well. But good news in this sense has the drawback that it is good only for some people, our good news was the worst of bad news for people in Germany and Japan – and that it is apt to be followed by news that isn't so good. So it is that only a few years after we again listen in to the news with apprehension and without much expectation of anything good.

The only good news in the history of the world that has been good for all men, and not in danger of being revised by subsequent happenings, is the news that was first whispered incredulously very early one Sunday morning in a Syrian garden, and taken up with growing confidence by the little group of people who knew what it meant. Today that news is repeated triumphantly all over the world in countless tongues. 'He is risen.' Every year as we sing our Easter hymns we share with millions of people in an experience which triumphs over history and geography. We are united with Christians of all ages, and also with Christians of all nations and colours. This is good news for Japanese and Germans, for Jews and Arabs, for men of India and of Pakistan, for people on the other side of the Iron Curtain as well as for us on this side. And nothing that anyone can do can shake it.

What is there about this far-off historical happening? Why should it lift the hearts of men everywhere all over the face of the earth, and without interval down 2,000 years of recorded history? After all, it is an event which Christians celebrate not once a year, but once a week. The Jews regarded Saturday as their holy day, but the Christians substituted Sunday because it was the day on which Jesus rose from the dead, and every Sunday the bells ring throughout Christendom in celebration of that fact. Why? Was it really as important as all that?

Its importance cannot be measured. It is the core of Christianity because it delivered mankind from the two oldest nightmares, each of which can paralyse a man's will and make nonsense of his efforts to live the good life. The first of these nightmares is fear of death. As long as man has been capable of recording his deepest fears and feelings he has recorded this fear. The haunting nightmare that he and all his works are doomed to be snuffed out and to become as if they had never been. What is the good of all our efforts if the grave is the goal? What is the value of human love and friendship, of beauty and truth and goodness, of all the things which give splendour and meaning to life, if the whole truth about man is that he is made of dust and returns to dust? These are the questions which have vexed man throughout his recorded history and there is a tremendous body of literature to show how agonizing the nightmare has been. And what has really tortured the most sensitive of men has been the thought of the futility of it all: we have immortal longings in us, an urge to survive, a conviction that there must be some sequel to the story. What a pitiable farce it is if all those longings are really meaningless and we are mocked by our own instincts.

'The last enemy is death.' People use that phrase as if it meant that death provides the final assault which no-one can withstand; they use the word 'last' in this context in the same sense as in the phrase 'the last straw'. But that is not how Paul used it. He used it in the sense in which we speak of getting into the last round, the final preliminary to victory. The last enemy *to be destroyed* is death.

The Christian message is that death has been destroyed. We ought to preach it more often. It means that the nightmare is at an end. No life is futile, however short or tragically cut-off: there will be a sequel. No separation is final; the Christian may mourn with restraint the loss of those whom he loves because he has the assurance that he will see them again. He is assured of that because in the grey of the early morning a tomb was found empty and the man who had been put there walked with his friends and talked to them. No wonder we call this good news. It matters to all of us, partly because at some time we all have to summon new faith in the face of bereavement, and also because, in facing the ordeal of life, it makes all the difference to know that we are preparing ourselves and being prepared for something beyond this existence. Keats called the world 'a vale of soul-making': that makes sense when we have the Christian faith of a destiny for the soul beyond the confines of this world.

The other nightmare from which Easter delivers us is the fear, which every good man feels in moments of depression, that evil may in the end prove stronger than good and that the last word may lie with the devil. Every man, however good he may be, has his breaking point, and civilizations have their breaking point too. In 'King Lear', the Earl of Gloucester, after a series of appalling experiences, threw in his hand and said: 'As flies to wanton boys are we to the Gods: they kill us for their sport.' By that he meant that evil is stronger than good, and we fight against it in vain.

Many modern writers have fallen into the same despair: Thomas Hardy, for instance, who saw God as a pitiless President of the Immortals, or H. G. Wells, who came to view the human species as doomed to be destroyed by its own stupidity.

There must be many people in the world today who are in the grip of this nightmare. Think of people in Czechoslovakia and Poland and Hungary and China, who have believed in such fruits of Christian civilization as justice, freedom and truth. As they suffer a tyranny which daily invades more and more of their lives, do you think that it is easy for them to go on believing that the ultimate principle of things is good and that goodness will prevail in the end?

What of our own experience? We have all had our moments of vision, when we caught a glimpse of the men we might be, and we have all had our moments of effort when we have tried to live up to our visions. But our record on the whole is one of failure: we have failed to do the things that we tried to do, and we have often done the things that we hated doing. And so we all of us, I suppose, suffer our moments of despondency and pessimism, when we feel that goodness is for other people, but evil is too strong for us.

Every Sunday morning comes with the same message to us all, whether our pessimism is caused by outside tyranny – that is, the material power of evil – or by the manifest failure of our own spiritual effort. And that message is 'Christ is risen.' All the immense resources of evil were mobilized against Him. The devil had no reserves by the time that Good Friday was over. Everything that evil could do had been thrown in against Him. The power of Imperial Rome could not prevail against Him: nor can the power of Marxist Russia, nor of capitalist America, nor of materialistic Britain. The nasty, common, little sins of ordinary people, the sins that we have in ourselves – cowardice, envy, ambition, dishonesty – these all helped to nail Him to the cross, but they couldn't keep Him there: nor can your sins and mine.

'Christ is risen.' He has triumphed over evil on the stage of world history; He has triumphed over evil in the area of the human heart. All men share in His victory, and nothing in earth or heaven or hell can turn the good news into bad news. The gates of hell shall not prevail against it.

There is a good deal of pessimism and defeatism in the world in which you and I have to live. The world is still incredulous about the Good News: it is still afraid of death and of the triumph of evil. What is needed more than anything is realistic optimism: not the shallow optimism of wishful thinking, but the confidence which is rooted in a courageous faith in the reality of the Good News of Easter. It is our job, if we are Christian, to carry about with us the infection of a good courage, for the last enemy has been overcome; the power of sin has been broken. Christ is risen, not merely in historical fact, but in everyday experience.

A SERMON PREACHED AT A MEMORIAL SERVICE FOR AN OLD RYDALIAN KILLED IN A FLYING ACCIDENT

'The last enemy that shall be destroyed is death.'
I Corinthians XV, 26

No-one, I am sure, would wish for a formal sermon this morning and I am not going to attempt one. I am going to ask you to join with me in facing squarely the mystery of this great calamity which we mourn, and in trying to see if there is any light in the darkness. Death is a fact about which we do not often think; now it has forced itself upon us. There are only two attitudes which men can possibly have towards this fact of Death: we may face it, or we may attempt to ignore it. But there are times – this is one of them – when the alternative is denied to us and we have no choice but to face this last enemy with what fortitude our religion or philosophy of life can afford us. Thank God that we meet here today as Christians with a Christian hope, knowing that the final power of the last of all enemies has been destroyed.

There are some people who, face to face with a tragedy of this kind, are able to bow their heads in patient resignation and say: 'Thy will be done.' But there must be many among you who would passionately reject this kind of attitude. Can we really believe that this appalling accident was the will of God for those whom we mourn and for their dear ones? Does God really will the loss and the suffering which have so suddenly come upon us? Is that the kind of God that He is? I want to say as emphatically as I can that I believe that such questions are fully justified: I do not believe for one moment that He is that kind of God. I do not believe that this sad catastrophe was part of His plan, but an accident in a world which He has created, not as a vast machine

67

obedient in every detail to a fixed, pre-ordained plan, but as a place in which His children enjoy the priceless gift of freedom – a gift which brings with it pain as well as pleasure and tears as well as laughter. But I am equally convinced that God is not defeated by any of the changes and chances of Life. With our limited vision we can see only the broken pieces of the pattern, but He patiently gathers that which has been scattered and He will bring good even out of evil. The great chaos into which our world is now plunged was never in God's purpose for it, but we believe that behind and beyond it He is working His purpose out and we know that in the end He will not be defeated nor His plans frustrated. The garden at Gethsemane and the cross at Calvary were not the will of God for His son. That was what the world which He had made did to God in the very teeth of His will. But out of that greatest of all evils He brought the most sublime good that the sons of men have known: the darkness of the crucifixion is shot through with the light of the resurrection, and as it was with Our Lord so it is with His servants whom we now mourn. He has overcome the world, and the last enemy whose final power He destroyed was Death.

Nothing is easier than to speak glibly of the comfort of prayer, but every Christian of experience knows that God is very near to those who call on Him in the extremity of their need. In our bewilderment and blindness, if we will put our hand into the darkness, we shall clasp the hand of God. And as we think of those on whom this blow has fallen most heavily, the parents and relatives and closest friends of the boys of whom we are thinking, let us remember that if we will we may make available for them mysterious sources of spiritual strength by prayers offered in faith and sincerity on their behalf. 'More things are wrought by prayer than this world dreams of.' If we are Christians we are sure that that is true, no matter how difficult we find it to pray. That is a service which we can all render, if we will, and it is impossible to measure the spiritual consequences of such prayer. 'The effectual, fervent prayer of a righteous man availeth much.'

This, then, is the light in our darkness, and these are the grounds for our hope: that this tragic disaster, though never willed by God, will in His infinite wisdom be turned to some good end in His eternal purposes; that this apparent waste of life will, in the Divine scheme, prove the opening of a door to a wider sphere of service; that the prayer of faith will bring comfort and strength to endure to those who suffer and mourn. These things we know, not because of any theories of men, but because God has pledged them and Christ has proved them.

Someone may say: 'These are only words, and words are easily spoken.' Let me add one thing more. Such words as these are not easily spoken, nor is it by any easy process that men come to believe them. Three years ago a very close friend of mine died in a motor accident. He was only twenty years of age, a man who combined to a rare degree lofty principles with a strong character and force of personality. He seemed marked out for a position of great influence for good, and many years of useful service to God and man – and because a mechanic had neglected to fasten a couple of screws he was picked up from the road-side on Newmarket Road and died in a few hours in Addenbrooke's hospital. I was brought suddenly and without warning face to face with the problem of Death with which you and I are faced today. I have tried to outline to you the sources of comfort which came to me in that time of spiritual bewilderment and suffering. Let us pray for faith to believe that the things that are seen are passing, but the things that are unseen are eternal and let us commit our friends, and those whose mourning for them is most intimate, and ourselves, to God our Father, whose Wisdom is as great as His Love. For we are all in the hands of the Living God, and He will never leave us nor forsake us.

A SERMON FOR REMEMBRANCE SUNDAY

There are many people, I know, who think that it is no longer appropriate that we should have Remembrance Services or observe the Two-Minutes' Silence. They argue that, after twenty years, such ceremonies have very little meaning, and that, with every year that passes, what we observe is more and more an empty ritual. It may be that many of you hold that view, and you are certainly entitled to. It is quite certain that it is the opinion of your generation that is going to determine whether or not this anniversary is going to be observed very much longer. I should like to spend a few moments in telling you, very simply, the kind of things that I find it relevant to think about in a service like this.

I have heard people allege, quite absurdly, that Remembrance Day represents some kind of glorification of war. That kind of thing could be said only by those who have forgotten – or have never known – what it is all about. For what we remember, above all else, is people whom we knew, who died when they had only just begun to live, and whose death has left us all immeasurably impoverished. We are annually reminded of the ghastly waste of war, which destroys, on an enormous scale, material which can never be replaced. And we think it right to remind you, who cannot remember them, of what they did for you, as well as for us.

Now is it true, as some people say, that these Services are a kind of patriotic pageant, glorifying the military history of the nation, in a museum which is no longer tolerable. For those men whom we remember died for a cause greater than any single country. When all the propaganda has been snipped away, and all the hindsight of historians, the simple fact remains that European civilization was threatened by a revival of pagan tyranny, and what had to be defended were the simple essentials – the freedom of men to speak their minds, and to choose their rulers, their freedom to worship, or not to worship, and justice, and the fundamental dignity of humanity. These things existed imperfectly before the war, and they exist today, still imperfectly, it is true, but the vision of them endures and their influence is growing; but no-one can doubt that they would have been swallowed up for generations, in another Dark Age, if they had not been defended.

Those men, whose names you see on the tablet outside this chapel, in the nature of things are only names to you, but we should not be here now but for them and thousands like them. Isn't it fitting that we should remember them? And remembering them, let us remember this, too; that concepts like freedom and justice and human dignity, are values which cannot be had cheaply. They were established in our tradition at great cost; they were defended and preserved, within living memory, at great cost; and we shall retain them, and hand them on to the future, only at great cost. So what I have to say to you is that this service should mean to us, not vague sentimentality, still less a kind of patriotic nostalgia, but obligation. Others were called on to die and we are called on to live, but the cause is the same.

The other thought that I find appropriate in this service is that of human interdependence; we are all members of one another. It is very fashionable, at present, for the inheritors of our civilization to deplore their inheritance, and blame their predecessors for it. If some writers are to be believed, a whole generation is plunged into self-pity, because it has to live in a world full of problems, menaced by atomic destruction, and international unrest, by colour problems and over-population and under-nourishment. All this is true. But we ought to be encouraged to think also of the great gifts that we have inherited. The standard of living of your generation is higher than that of any previous age; your expectation of life and health is greater; your opportunities of education and the riches of a scientific age are things which surpass the wildest dreams of every other age. Let us take time off from grumbling at our forefathers and let us be grateful to them for the good things that we enjoy without having earned them.

It is easier to feel resentment than gratitude, because resentment feeds our pride and our self-confidence, but gratitude makes us admit our dependence on others and calls for humility. And it is fitting that we should be humble and grateful, as we remember in this service the men whose sacrifice meant that we could live in relative peace and freedom, instead of in violence and slavery.

One last thing remains to be said. Of course the men who died did not *secure* the things which they defended. Those things are never secured once and for all. What they did was to give *us* the opportunity to serve the same causes; to build a society in which men may live the good life and find the Kingdom of God. Our society today doesn't look very much like that. It is full of materialism and self-seeking; of crime and violence; it has many virtues, but it is characterized by much that is cheap and slick. Its values are in doubt. It has lost its faith and its vision.

And this Remembrance Service, if it has any relevance today and is not, indeed, an empty ritual, speaks to our condition. It reminds us of the simple things that really are the cement of society; duty, compassion, and doing the will of God. It reminds us of our privileges; of the things that we enjoy through the sacrifice of others; of our obligation to preserve and increase those values for those who come after.

'I am come that they may have life.

'You are not your own; you are bought with a price. Freely you have received; freely give.'

A SERMON ON SUFFERING

I am going to speak this morning on the subject of the Christian answer to the problem of suffering. This is a difficult topic to talk about and I have chosen it only because I was asked last term to do so. It may be that some people will feel that it is not a very suitable subject for a school chapel, but suffering in some form comes to all of us sooner or later and it is good that we should know, if possible before the crisis comes to us, what is the teaching of our religion on this burden which is common to the whole human race. It is a particularly necessary subject to face in these tragic days in which we live. During the holidays I read a letter in *Picture Post* which stated quite simply that the haphazard results of indiscriminate bombing made it quite impossible for us to go on believing in the existence of a benevolent God who loved us and took an interest in our lives. This letter combined a pathetic note of genuine suffering with a profound ignorance of religious truth: it is sheer blindness not to recognize that it is representative of the thinking of thousands of people today and that it is an attitude which needs to be met.

In speaking of suffering I am using the word in its widest sense to cover the afflictions and calamities which come upon men, often suddenly out of the blue, and which play havoc with their plans and with their lives: pain, accident, illness, bereavement and sorrow. The first fact that we need to recognize and face is that they happen to all men and do not come as a result of God's judgment on the way in which we are living our lives. That is a very common delusion. It is an idea which runs through the literature of the ancient world, and is to be found

73

prominently in many of the Psalms and in the Book of Job. Our first lesson was an example of it.

This idea was at the back of the disciples' minds when they asked Jesus whether the man had been born blind because of his own or his parents' sins. And Jesus answered 'Neither'. But thousands of people today still believe the same thing, and when the blow comes to them their first question is: 'Why did this have to happen to *me*?' We have a sort of blind feeling that misfortune should come only to the wicked and that virtuous people – people like ourselves – should somehow be exempt from it. But the world is manifestly not run like that: anyone who knows anything of the suffering which has arisen from this war knows that.

The fact is that suffering is an inevitable consequence of freedom: if we value the one we must accept the other. No doubt God could have made a world in which a race of automata automatically did the right things because a terrible doom instantaneously fell upon them if they didn't, but that is not the sort of world which in fact He did make and in which we have to live. He made us free, to do good or to do evil, and we have to face the consequences, not only of our own choice, but of other people's. In other words God made a world for adult human beings, not a nursery for infants.

Perhaps an illustration will make this clearer. When you were an infant your parents kept you as safe as they could from accident. Whenever you went out of doors some grown-up person went with you. If you wanted to cross the road you did it in a sort of convoy. But the time had to come when you went out alone to face the hazards of the highway. If you had been injured by a careless motorist that would have been an accident which befell you, not because your parents had ceased to love you, but because in their wisdom they had allowed you the risk of freedom, knowing that without that risk you could never develop your own personality or – as we say – grow up. Your parents might have chosen to shelter and spoon-feed you all your days: they might have prevented you from riding a bicycle or refrained from sending you away to school, but in so doing they would have deprived you, not only of the danger of suffering, but also of all chance of happiness and development. They chose otherwise. God might have made a world of helpless, sheltered infants, free from all danger and devoid of all independence and personality, but He chose otherwise. And if we value our freedom then we must accept as its condition the chance of suffering, brought upon us, not only by our own wrong choices and folly, but also by those of others.

This war came upon the world as a result of the evil ambitions of our enemies and as a result, too, of the apathy and laziness of our own statesmen and people. The price has had to be paid by thousands of innocent men and women. Many people said in 1939 'Why didn't God strike down Hitler and so make the war impossible?' The answer is that if God struck down everyone whom He saw meditating or committing evil none of us would survive this judgment. We live in a world in which we may both enjoy unmerited benefits from the goodness of others and suffer undeserved harm from their sins: we need to remember that it is also true that other people suffer harm from our own evil-doing. It is open to us to imagine in our arrogance that we could have made a better world, but that is the kind of world that God has made and we had better accept it.

There is nothing particularly Christian about this: any courageous pagan could say as much. Henley, for instance, said it when he wrote:

It matters not how strait the gate
How charged with punishment the scroll:
I am the master of my fate
I am the captain of my soul.

The Christian can go much further than that. There are two considerations which I want to add and I can sum them up quite briefly.

The first is that, as Christians, we believe that God Himself accepted the conditions of the world that He had made. In the person of Jesus Christ He lived on the same terms as you and I. He knew pain and sorrow and bereavement, fear and anxiety and ultimately death. God is not what the pagans believed Him to be: a remote or amused spectator of man's tortured struggles in a bewildering world. He has

75

shared in our drama and known the bitterness of the cup which He prayed should pass from Him. When Jesus wept over the city of Jerusalem as it chose spiritual death and rejected Him; when He agonized in the garden of Gethsemane and knew the final loneliness and isolation of the Cross He was revealing to us the true nature of God. The cross is not only an incident in the history of the world: it is an eternal truth about its Creator. The sufferings of His creatures do not leave Him unmoved: in the words of the apostle: 'We have not a high priest who is untouched by the feeling of our infirmities, but as He has suffered He is able to succour.' We are often told in these days by shallow thinkers that all religions are in essence the same thing, but this is not true. The Christian faith is the only one which has at its heart a God who suffers with and for His people, that they may accept the conditions of life without bitterness and without whining.

Finally, the Christian is taught to believe that the last word does not lie with the misfortune that comes upon him. The human spirit has at its disposal resources upon which it can call in adversity and which will enable it to rise triumphant over apparent disaster. A little more than twenty years ago a rising young politician was suddenly attacked by infantile paralysis: for four years he lay in bed – a helpless invalid and everyone except himself believed that his active career was over. But last month the whole civilized world mourned that man's death as the death of a statesman to whom the democratic cause owes a debt that cannot be measured. The story of Roosevelt's life is the story of a man who refused to be crushed by disaster: out of apparent defeat he was able to bring victory, just as John Milton wrote the best of all his poetry not in the prime of his successful public life, but when the cause in which he believed had gone down in defeat and he himself had been stricken with total blindness. And both these great men had in common a deep-rooted faith in God.

The Christian religion stands for the triumph of goodness over all evil, including the evil of suffering. To the Roman empire the Cross was the symbol of degradation and disgrace – it was a gibbet or a gallows: it stood for brutality in its crudest form. Jesus turned it into the symbol of mercy and of charity. In a world of war it has often been the only sign of human kindliness: hundreds of repatriated prisoners have testified that in their captivity their only source of hope and comfort was that society which has as its emblem the Red Cross. We do well to remind ourselves that if it had not been for the sufferings and triumph of our Lord there would never have been any Red Cross with all that it means and the civilized world might have gone down long since in a welter of barbarism.

The Christian knows that the afflictions which come upon him and upon those whom he mourns are only temporary sufferings which will pass away with the world to which they belong. The last word about him will be spoken by the God who is his Father, so that with a courage that is rooted in faith he awaits the day when God shall wipe away all tears from all eyes. What other faith or philosophy of life is there that can match the need of the distracted world in which we live?

'THY KINGDOM COME'

Matthew VI, 10

During your time at this school you cannot have failed to notice that
we attach a great deal of importance to worship and to attending services. When the time comes for you to leave – and it is drawing very
near for a good many of you – it is only natural that, amongst the
mixed feelings with which you greet such a milestone in your lives,
you should look forward to not having to do some of the things which
you have to do at school: you may even have a list of such things
already drawn up in your mind. Anyone who knows the values in
which Rydal is rooted must be concerned that you should not include,
among the expendable things, this habit of regular worship. I want to
talk this morning about the Christian Church and what I believe to be
our duty to it. Remember, it is more, far more, than the school chapel,
or the two churches with which we are associated in this town. It was
started by Jesus himself to preserve his gospel in the world: in spite of
efforts to stamp it out it has survived to stand by the grave of its
persecutors. And we believe that when the last word has been written
in the story of man this church, alone amongst the enterprises of
mankind, will remain and endure.

I am going to suggest to you that it is the duty of everyone who
calls himself a Christian to belong to one or other of the churches and
to express his loyalty to Christ in loyalty to that Church. It is not for
me to say which church it should be: that is likely to be decided by your
upbringing and temperament and other considerations of the kind. But

I am going to try to meet some of the objections which are commonly made when people are asked to give of their time and their energy in the service of any church.

Most of these objections are expressed in terms of criticism. I have often talked with people who have defended their neglect of the church in the holidays or after they had left school, in this sort of way. They have said that the building is very ugly, or the music bad, or the preaching worse than bad; that the congregation is very small, that no other young people go and so on. Sometimes the criticism is wider, and vaguer: they say that the church has failed, that the church is out of date, that the church has nothing to say to the modern generation.

Now of course anyone who doesn't call himself a Christian has a perfect right to take up this position. But I don't see how a Christian or anyone who would like to be a Christian can make use of any of these arguments. To begin with, if you think that there is something wrong with the Church – and there is a great deal wrong with all of them – the right place from which to criticize them is inside and not outside. It's no good saying that the *Church* is old-fashioned: what you mean is that the people who go to church are old-fashioned, but if you won't go there and tell them how to talk to your generation how can the church be anything else? It won't do to sit at home grumbling about one standard of preaching and the quality of the music, as though a service were a concert or an exhibition of elocution. The Christian attitude to worship is that we go to church to give as well as to receive and it may be that the services in your church are failing for lack of exactly the kind of contribution that you could make to them. But this at least is certain: any criticisms that you may direct at the church from outside will be destructive, negative and entirely useless. No-one will take any notice of your suggestions unless you and thousands more of your generation are prepared to take off your coats and join in and help to implement your criticisms. It is a sound human instinct to mistrust the detached critic. If you were engaged in any practical task, such as building a boat or rehearsing an oratorio, how much notice would you take of a man who stood by with his hands in his pockets and told you that you were doing it all wrong? You would invite him either to join in and do better or to go somewhere else. And the church wants its non-co-operative critics to join in.

There is no need for me to enumerate the faults from which the churches suffer. Every thoughtful Christian admits them and laments them. But most of them spring from the weakness of organized Christianity and that weakness could be remedied if the people who believe in the fundamental truths for which the churches stand would rally to their support. I know that there are hundreds, probably thousands, of good men who pray and work for the coming of the Kingdom of God and who stand aloof from organized Christianity: I know that they are sincere but I honestly believe them to be wrong. Such people owe everything that they value to the fact that there has been a Christian Church in history. It is enough to say that but for that organization we should have had no Bible with all that it means in the history of the world, and particularly of European civilization. Think what the Christian tradition has meant in the development of our own British tradition and in that of the Americans: we owe our tradition to the faithful Christian Church which preserved the light undimmed through the Dark Ages, when all the other lights went out, to the teaching of that church through centuries of ignorance, and to the Authorized Version of the Bible from which in the last three hundred years, we have derived more than we can ever trace. But for the Christian Church, I say, there could have been no Christian tradition. Such is our legacy from the past. What kind of values can we hope to hand on to the future if we abandon that organization which has been the channel of everything that we have come to value most lightly?

In one of his books Mr C. S. Lewis speaks of the world as an occupied country, dominated by the powers of evil which have no right to be there. As you look around the world today there is a good deal of evidence in support of the analogy. Envy, hatred and the lust for power are abroad in the world and in every country there are the quislings who have thrown in their lot with the powers of darkness. I remember talking to a Yorkshire miner some years ago. He lived in a depressed area and had been unemployed for years. He had already told me that he had no use for religion and rejected the word 'sin' when I used it as being meaningless. Then the talk turned to politics and he proclaimed fiercely that all the parties were as bad as each other; and all politicians shamelessly on the make. 'The only problem,' he said to me 'is human selfishness.' I hadn't the heart to tell him that he had produced a perfect definition of that mysterious word 'sin'.

Of course he was right, but to state a problem is not the same thing as to solve it. We need to recognize when we pray 'Thy Kingdom come' that the chief obstacle to the coming of God's Kingdom is selfishness – our own and other people's: that is the Fifth Column amongst us which makes a mockery of our prayers and delivers our country into the hands of the powers of evil.

C. S. Lewis's analogy is a good one: the New Testament constantly employs military metaphors in speaking of the spiritual conflict. Those people who have chosen their side and desire to fight as well as pray for the coming of the Kingdom of God would do well to throw in their lot with the force which is organized to fight for that objective – I mean the Christian Church.

If the Germans had invaded this country how much help to our defence would have come from isolated defenders indulging in individual guerilla warfare in the hills? In the spiritual struggle how much help are those who stand aloof from the forces which, however faulty their organization, have championed the cause for nearly 2,000 years and never been driven out of the field?

'The Bible,' said Wesley, 'knows nothing of a solitary religion.' Our Lord entrusted his work, not to scattered individuals, but to a solid group, for he knew, even if we don't, our need of one another. Since then the church has passed through many critical days, but never, as I believe, has her task been greater than it is today. We like to speak of this as a Christian country: we do well to remember that out of every ten people in Great Britain nine belong to no church at all. That is the measure of the task which confronts Christian men today, and if it is to be undertaken we must say goodbye to disunion and to easy criticism. One thing is certain: if your generation fails her then the Church must fail to rise to the opportunities of the present – and who knows what

81

dark ages the world will have to endure before such opportunities come again?

It may be, after all, that all these heroic military metaphors are misleading: it may be that your Christian duty at this moment of crisis is to do something very dull and prosaic: to attend a church where the music offends your ear and the preaching outrages your intelligence and to give your time and energy to putting life into an apathetic and not very numerous congregation. Some quite insignificant person used to teach in a certain Scottish Sunday School and the work must often have seemed dull and unimportant, but David Livingstone was in the class and a new continent was opened up as a result. And in Browning's words, if we do our duty as we see it: 'God surely will contrive use for our earning.'

When we pray 'Thy Kingdom come' let us pray also that we may be shown how we can help to answer our own prayer.

'EXCEPT THE LORD BUILD THE HOUSE THEY LABOUR IN VAIN THAT BUILD IT'

Psalm CXXVII, 1

We are all very preoccupied with the question of building at the present time, and this is only natural. A time of significant extension in the amenities of a school is a moment of importance in its development and life. But we ought to remind ourselves that a building is, at best, only a means to an end, and it is fitting that at this time we should remember the ends which this school exists, and has always existed, to serve.

The scope of education is seen today to be wider than ever before. It is not only a matter of training the mind through studies, and the body through athletic pursuits, and the talents and interests through an ever-increasing variety of activities; education is concerned, we know now, with the whole man and we have to train, not only the *individual*, with his unique equipment, but also the *person*, with his place in society and his duty to other people. These things are commonplaces of educational theory.

But there is something else which goes deeper than all this and which we derive, not from up-to-date educational thought, but from the theory and practice of our Founder. It is expressed in the words of our text: 'Except the Lord build the house . . . they labour in vain.' This means, quite simply, that we exist as a school to do the will of God, and that if we fail to do that we might as well not exist at all. It is good that we should try to equip people, academically and in other ways, to play their part in the world in which they have to live, but this is good only because it is part of the will of God: it is highly desirable that we should improve our amenities and extend our premises, but it is desirable only in order that we may fulfil better our task of doing the will of God. Rydal was founded as a Christian school. The man who started it, and the men who have maintained its tradition over the years, have not only been faithful in building: they have been staunch in the faith that the Lord was building, and that their labour was therefore not in vain.

Let us be quite clear what this implies. The first step in any building is the drawing of the plans, by which all the work is shaped and conditioned. And when we apply this text to the life of our school we are implying that God has a plan for us and that, if we are not to build in vain, we must build in accordance with that plan.

Do we, in fact, believe this or do we only say it? Most people in this complicated age have no such simple faith. Whatever men may say, it is a fact which you can observe in the contemporary scene, that most people live their lives as if we were at the mercy of random forces like chance, or as if the plans of powerful men were all that we had to take account of. Many people have actually reverted to a kind of fatalism. They really believe that there are certain forces in history which are guiding the destiny of our race in a certain direction, and that there is nothing that anyone can do about it.

But our belief is quite different. We believe that God has a plan, that safety and happiness for mankind consist in living in accordance with it and that ruin and disaster, in the end, are the lot of those who ignore it. How could it be otherwise? The history of our race is littered with the wreckage of civilizations and empires which built arrogantly according to the will of man, but the Lord did not build the house, and so they laboured in vain. We have seen it happen in our own lifetime. Hitler announced in 1940, after his lightning campaign in Europe, that he had settled the future of Europe for the next 1,000 years – and it looked at the time as if he might be right. Yet within five years the whole structure had crashed around him. The Lord had not built the house and they laboured in vain.

There is much food for thought here, in regard both to our school and to the wider question of society without. It has its relevance in the ethics of business, in international relationships, in questions of race and colour and class. In all man's relationships with man God has his will and his purpose for our behaviour and the only thing that ultimately matters is that we should find out that will and do it. This is a very simple view of life: it would revolutionize every department if we applied it. We have to seek to apply it in the affairs of this school.

I want to add that this is also true of our individual lives. When we were children and played with bricks, we used to pile them aimlessly on one another and see what the structure looked like at the end. But as we grew older we came to a better kind of building – perhaps modelling something from a blueprint, or drawing from a model, but in any case we learned the lesson of craftsmanship which is that we can labour constructively only in obedience to a plan which has been chosen.

This development is a kind of picture of what happens in the larger issues of life. Up to a certain point your education consists of a lot of pieces of more or less unrelated knowledge and bits of experience. Then you reach an age at which you can fit them into some kind of pattern. Then you specialize in certain related subjects, perhaps because you have decided on a career, which means that you have hit on a master-plan into which everything now has to fit.

As a Christian school it is our duty to proclaim that, not only has God a plan and a purpose for the traditions of this place which are entrusted to us, but he also has a purpose for every separate person passing through the school. We can say, not only of the fabric of our buildings and of the stuff of our traditions, but also of every career which is planned and shaped here: 'Except the Lord build the house they labour in vain that build it.'

Religion is a far bigger thing than we like to admit. We have developed a technique for confining it to a department of our lives. We have special clothes in which to indulge in it and a separate day of the week on which to practice it. But if God comes into our lives He will not be so restricted. He is interested in our work and our play, our skills and our hobbies, our friendships and our vocation. The way in which we spend our lives matters to Him. Many a man has lived an outwardly prosperous life and has achieved what the world calls success, but he has known in his heart that the real verdict on his career is failure, because the Lord did not build in his life and his labour has been in vain.

There is one more thing, of the greatest importance, to say. The Lord does not only supply a plan for what we build; he makes available for us his power and help in the work of building. That is the heart of the Christian gospel. We are not left to do the will of God in our strength. Just as He came into the world in the person of his son, to reveal his will and his way, so he comes into the world and into the experience of men in the person of his spirit to enable us to obey him. During the American Civil War an anxious lady said to Abraham Lincoln: 'Do you think that the Lord is on our side?' He answered, 'I don't know, madam, but I hope that we are on his.' The difference is important. So often we make our plans and then ask God to bless them, but his purpose is that we should first find out his will and then seek, in his strength, to do it. In this faith let us build in our school and in our own lives, that our labour may not be in vain.

A SERMON PREACHED AT THE END OF THE
SUMMER TERM – JULY 1964

'That these things that cannot be shaken may remain'
Hebrews XII, 27

You will expect me to begin with a reminder which is commonplace at this stage of the School year. For many of you this is the last service that you will ever attend as members of this school; for all of you it is a significant time in your school career. What is left of the education that you have experienced, or endured, during the days which have led up to this day? Especially for those of you for whom this *is* an end of a kind, what is left and what will be left? Certainly a great deal will be forgotten – Algebra and Latin; details in many subjects, whole outlines in subjects which you gave up at one stage or another in your ascent. The whole pattern of your life here has been made up of things which have made their own appropriate contribution to one stage of your development, but many of which you may never do again. But some things, surely, will remain with you after four or five of the most impressionable years of your life. The things that cannot be shaken will remain. What are they and what ought they to be?

These are questions which are answered less confidently today than they used to be. At one time I think, not so very long ago, people had a very clear vision of the educational aim. A classical education gave them a picture of life which had commended itself to the best minds of the ancient and modern world. Add to that a conventional acceptance of what was generally agreed to be the Christian behaviour, together with the ethics of the games field, the conduct of a gentleman, and the picture was more or less complete. But none of these values has survived unchallenged into the contemporary world.

The classics gave way to science and for a short time it seemed that our kind of certainty had been replaced by another, but this has not proved true. People no longer speak confidently, as they once did, of the certainties of science, or an evolution which is automatic progress and so on. The scientist holds his hypothesis only until a better one comes along and takes its place, and truth is divided and subdivided by the sciences into so many compartments that many people have given up looking for any coherent pattern.

On the ordinary level of life this atmosphere of uncertainty has become part of the air that we breathe. Doubt has become the characteristic accent in which even religious leaders speak: doubt about what we ought to believe, doubt about how we ought to behave, doubt about where we came from and where we are going. The old signposts have been discredited, it seems: the old landmarks have gone: life is not a Pilgrim's Progress, but a blind man's buff. Where everything is a matter of opinion, how may we know the truth? Where everything is relative and subject to change, what are the things that cannot be shaken? To make it very personal and topical, what are the things that I hope will be characteristic of people who have passed through this place, things that will remain when logarithms and Latin verbs are as much things of the past as long runs and gated assemblies? I will name three things and I will speak of them fairly briefly, though each is a subject that is inexhaustible.

The first thing that I covet for you is a sense of duty. I know that that is a very drab and old-fashioned thing to talk about: duty is lacking in glamour, and it doesn't appear much in the headlines, and the people who make most money are perhaps not always those who value duty most highly. But it is a simple fact of experience that the world is kept going by men who have a sense of obligation. They make civilization possible, they maintain the fabric of the world and it is on their backs that the line-shooters and the glib flashy men in the headlines travel through life. There are two attitudes from which you can choose as you journey through the world. One is summed up in the title of a book: 'The world owes me a living.' The other is summed up as a sense of obligation. It is the people who know that they are debtors to the past, and that they have to repay that debt to the present and the future, who are the salt of the earth and the light of the world, and this value is one of the things that cannot be shaken.

The illustration of it lies ready to hand in your own recent experience. Everyone here will agree with me when I say that our life here has been enriched enormously in the last six weeks by the new swimming bath; no-one will want to argue about that. Where did the bath come from? It came from the generosity of parents and of old boys. Now why should an Old Rydalian give money to provide a swimming bath for a school of which he is no longer a member? Does the Old Rydalians' Club owe us a swimming bath? It's too late to be of any use to them. But many an Old Rydalian knows, however dimly, that he enjoyed amenities in his day which had been given to him by his predecessors and so he pays his debt to the past in the only way in which it can be paid – he pays it to the future.

It is this attitude towards life that I covet as a distinguishing mark of those who have spent some time in this place. One of the best activities in the school is that in which some of us go out to do jobs for elderly people in the town. It isn't an activity to talk about a lot, or to feel self-consciously virtuous about, but those of you who have done a bit of it will know that it carries its own reward – not, I hope, in any sunny self-righteousness, but in the feeling that this is the kind of thing that we are meant to do. Freely you have received: freely give. After all, we are all people who have been given a pretty good start in life, relatively speaking. You may or may not want to express it in religious terms and talk about loving your neighbour, but this sense of obligation is the first of the things that cannot be shaken which I hope that you will carry through life, here or elsewhere.

Secondly, duty to God. I expect that only some of you will agree with me when I say that duty to your neighbour and duty to God are two conceptions which are indispensable to one another. But I am sure that it is true. Of course there are plenty of people who do good to their neighbours without calling themselves religious men or talking about

God. They may even call themselves agnostics and imagine that they don't believe in God. But if they really believe that they have an inescapable obligation to serve others, and if they go on doing so even when it is inconvenient and troublesome, then it is evident that they believe in something absolute beyond themselves. They may call it duty and spell it with a capital D, but they are doing the will of God and they are to be commended, as the Good Samaritan was commended. He didn't make any profession of belief, you may remember, and he didn't talk religion, but he helped a man in need and Jesus said that we were to go and do the same.

But I hope that you will come to see a sense of obligation to God – to worship Him and try to find out His will and do it – as one of the unshakeable things that remain in the view of life that you have found here. A few Sundays ago a man stood in this pulpit whom we are privileged to see and hear every two years, when he comes back from the front line, where he fights in the spiritual war. He is a man whose character and integrity make all theoretical argument about goodness and religion look very cheap. Do you remember what Dr Haigh said about life in Nigeria – that the jobs that really need doing are done by the mugs and the mugs are those who believe in God? I have nothing really to say under this heading other than to remind you of that and to commend to you the example of that unpretentious missionary doctor, whose life is an illustration of the things that cannot be shaken. There is no Old Rydalian of whom we have more cause to be proud.

The last thing is this. Last month I heard a distinguished historian speaking in a television programme. He is not known as a particularly religious man – in the orthodox sense, but he said something about religion which I thought very helpful. He defined it as 'feeling pretty humble before the mystery'. I should hate to think that anyone could leave here unaware of the mystery – that he could go through life satisfied with a narrow little materialism, with both feet on the ground, and both eyes on the main chance, and no sense of eternity in his soul. There are times in life when we encounter beauty in Nature or in Art, or goodness in character or in action, and we hear somewhere (not with our ears) and we are aware of another dimension, the accents of an unknown idiom, the voice of Truth, incoherent but unmistakable. You can grow very insensitive to that sort of experience unless it is part of your way of life; one of the things that cannot be shaken.

All this is mystery; the freedom which comes through the sense of men and of God; the sense of God within the soul which we call awe; it is only in Jesus that the mystery becomes intelligible. Of all the things that cannot be shaken, our experience of Him is the key to everything else. We cannot give much meaning to the name of God unless we give it the meaning which He has taught us; we find Him and know Him in the acts of service and in the experience of mystery of which I have spoken. One of the greatest living Christians has spoken of our knowledge of Him in these words with which I close. 'He comes to us as one unknown, as of old He came to those who knew Him not. He speaks to us the same word, "Follow thou me", and He sets us to the task which He has to fulfil for our time. He commands. And to those who obey Him, be they wise or simple, He will reveal Himself... and as an ineffable mystery they shall learn, in their own experience, who HE is.'

A SERMON PREACHED AT THE END OF THE
SUMMER TERM – JULY 16th, 1967

'And when he came to himself'

I want to talk about one of the most encouraging phrases that I know. It comes in the best-known short story in the world, which we wrongly call the Prodigal Son. It is really about God and the way in which he deals with men. This is the phrase: 'And when he came to himself.'

The word 'self', which sounds a simple enough word, really stands for something very complicated. Modern psychologists recognize that when they divide it into the Ego and the Super Ego and the Id, but long before such terms were invented men knew that the self is a many-sided thing. Of course, we all know it in our own experience, don't we? Over the oracle at Delphi where the Greeks used to go to try to find out the truth about life, there were written two words – KNOW THYSELF: the very fact that they appeared there, as a kind of motto, indicates that self-knowledge is something that we don't acquire very easily.

One of the tests that selection boards in the Army used to give to candidates for commissions was this: write two short essays, one describing yourself as your best friend sees you, and the other as your worst enemy sees you. Probably both the essays, if they were properly written, would include some truth, but two very different selves would emerge. Do you ever think about yourself and wonder what sort of person you really are? There is what we call our best self, the person that we would like to be. There is the self that your parents see and the self that appears on your school report or in a testimonial. There is also

92

perhaps the side of yourself that you know exists, though you wish that it didn't; the self that tells lies to get out of trouble; the self that does things in a crowd that it would never do alone; the self that is self-centred and unwilling to meet its obligations and honour its loyalties.

All this is in this marvellous parable. You can invent all sorts of excuses for the Prodigal Son: he was overshadowed by his elder brother and wanted to stand on his own feet, or something like that. The plain fact was that he was selfish, that he wanted his own way and that – like a lot of immature people, he thought that he must express himself by rebellion, whether there was anything to rebel about or not. So he went to his father and said to him two words which sum up a man's worst self – 'Give me'. What he was asking for was his inheritance. What he was saying in effect was, 'Father, I can't wait for you to die; you're taking too long about it. So give me my share of what's coming to me and I'll go off on my own.' There is no sign that he recognized any duty to his parents, any obligation to be grateful for his inheritance. He thought that the world owed him a living and his motto was: 'Give me.'

Now, of course, it is right that people, when they grow up, should leave home, but it is evident in the context that this young man's proper place for the moment was under his father's roof. Indeed, he proved that, by making such a fool of himself when he did get away. But the father was marvellously patient. He gave the boy what he wanted, without saying anything to him about duty and loyalty and obligation, and he left him free to learn the lesson that life was about to teach him.

We all know what happened. He went off to some swinging city, he got in with a crowd of people whose values were as low as those of his worst self, and then he made a complete mess of things. You will find out in life, if you haven't already, that a group of people can be far more wicked and cruel and stupid when they are together than any would be alone. That's what this boy found when he had wasted his substance in riotous living. His friends melted away because he was no use to them – they were as self-centred as he. The people who help you to be your worst self never are any use. He was penniless and destitute and – as the story grimly says – no man gave unto him. He got a job looking after someone else's pigs, which involved sharing their food.

It is at this point in the story that the words of my text occur – what I have referred to as one of the most encouraging phrases that I know – 'And when he came to himself'. Everything followed that ought to follow. He went home and apologized to his father and, just as his worst self was summed up in the words 'give me', his better self was summed up in the words 'make me'. 'Make me as one of your hired servants,' he said, because he could see that service gives a purpose in life which the self-centred never knows.

The world is made up of two kinds of people; those who say 'give me' and those who say 'make me' – those who want a purpose to live by and a cause to serve. And each of us is potentially one of these kinds or the other. We have to choose. And the encouraging thing in the parable is that God leaves us free to choose and that we have the capacity to make the right choice. 'And when he came to himself' it wasn't the selfish, immature rebel that he came to, but to the self which had acquired a true sense of values and of loyalty, the self of a man who knew where he truly belonged and had the humility and the guts to get up and go there.

I think that this is an important service. It is the last one for nearly a quarter of you: it is a milestone, because the end of a year, for all of you. No-one who preaches habitually in a school chapel expects that anything he says there will be remembered for very long by anyone. But if I could choose anything for you to associate this place with, and to base your lives on, it would be the two truths which emerge so plainly from this story, that Jesus told and men have never forgotten. First, that God trusts you with the freedom to make the choices which determine what your self is like and is going to be like; and second, that it is within the power of us all to realize our true selves, not by greed and self-seeking, but in the service of our God and of our fellow-men.

Experiments in Chapel

CAESAR'S FRIEND

The scene is the office of the Governor-General in a modern Pro-
tectorate. The Governor-General is talking on the phone as the
curtain rises. His A.D.C. sits and pretends not to listen. The Governor
is a middle-aged, experienced man, rather tired, a little cynical and very
civilized. The A.D.C. is youngish and professional.

GOVERNOR

Yes, dear, I've just finished the interrogation. What did I think of
him? Well, I was rather impressed to tell you the truth. Bit of a
fanatic, I suppose, from what they say about him, but a tremendous
personality. They're howling for his blood, but he doesn't seem a
bit rattled. No – a very cool customer. You'd have thought that *we*
were on trial really. I don't understand these people. What's that you
say? [*Pause, while he listens to something rather prolonged and urgent,
during which he makes a few appropriate noises.*] Yes. Well that's
very interesting, but it's hardly evidence. No, there's no danger of
anything drastic. An acquittal? Well, hardly. He's got some very
influential enemies. Something formal and face-saving I should
think. I say, I must hang up now, old girl, I've got a lot of work to
do. No, I won't be late. I *haven't* forgotten that we're playing bridge
tonight. No. Bridge with the General isn't an easy date to forget.
Goodbye. [*He hangs up and turns to his* A.D.C.] All right, Robert;
you can abandon that pose of non-attachment. There's nothing
more interesting than other people's telephone conversations is there?

A.D.C. [*rather perfunctorily – he isn't really embarrassed*]

No really, sir, I assure you –

GOVERNOR

You'll be a very good diplomat, but there's no need to practise on me. I'm a professional myself, so you won't fool me. That was my wife, as if you didn't know.

A.D.C.

I thought perhaps it was, sir.

GOVERNOR

Yes, she's very interested in the interrogation. She's got some kind of a hunch about the prisoner and she wants us to watch our step. Highly irregular and all that sort of thing, but there it is. You look as if you didn't approve.

A.D.C.

Not at all, sir. It's not for me to express an opinion.

GOVERNOR

You expressed one, with your eloquent eyebrows. You'll need to control them in the interests of your career.

A.D.C.

Yes, sir.

GOVERNOR

And don't be stuffy. As a matter of fact it's a good thing in our job to have a wife who takes an intelligent interest in what we have to do. You'd better remember that. Some of your blondes don't impress me in that capacity.

A.D.C.

Really, sir –

GOVERNOR

Oh. I know that you're still working through the qualifying rounds. But remember what I say when you get into the final.

[*There is a knock at the door.*]

See who that is, will you, Robert.

[*He picks up a letter and looks at it while the* A.D.C. *goes to the door. After a short quiet conversation with someone he comes back.*]

A.D.C.

It's the Archbishop, sir. They say he wants to see you urgently.

GOVERNOR

Good Lord. This means trouble. His Grace doesn't usually drop in without warning. Tell them to send him in.

[*The* A.D.C. *goes to the door and returns, in a moment, with the Archbishop. This is an elderly, but not old, cleric, who should be dressed in a way which suggests that he is a foreigner, but there must be no nonsense with broken English. He looks a shrewd capable man, more like the head of a great business concern than the leader of the Church.*]

GOVERNOR [*rising*]

How do you do, your Grace? It is always a pleasure to see you.

ARCHBISHOP

I'm sorry to come like this without warning. I hope that my visit is not inconvenient.

GOVERNOR

Not at all. I am always at your disposal.

[*The two men eye each other carefully, like chess players whose tactics depend on their appraisal of one another's intentions.*]

You know my A.D.C. Captain Cameron, I think.

ARCHBISHOP

Yes, of course. Good evening Captain.

A.D.C.

Good evening, sir.

GOVERNOR

Do you wish to speak to me in private, Archbishop?

ARCHBISHOP

I have nothing to say that Captain Cameron is not welcome to hear. It will be for you to decide.

GOVERNOR

Very well. I'll tell you, Robert, if I want you to go.

A.D.C.

Sir!

GOVERNOR

Let's sit down, shall we? Now, your Grace, what can I do for you?

ARCHBISHOP

You have recently concluded an interrogation, I believe?

99

GOVERNOR

Oh, are you interested in that agitator? I didn't realize that it was a
Church matter. Our inquiry was conducted strictly on a political
basis.

ARCHBISHOP

Yes. In your country, of course, political and religious matters are
kept in different compartments. That is not the case with us. Perhaps
it is because we take our religion more seriously – but that is not for
me to say. But it matters very much to us, in both contexts, that you
should not underestimate the danger which this man represents.

GOVERNOR

You take him seriously?

ARCHBISHOP

Very seriously.

GOVERNOR

And you have come to make sure that I take a firm line with him?

ARCHBISHOP

I have come to make sure that you put him to death.

[*The Archbishop makes this demand in a matter-of-fact way which is
all the more shocking for its lack of emphasis and there is a silence that
can be felt for a moment.*]

GOVERNOR

You must forgive me, but I find that a little difficult to understand. I
have just conducted an interrogation which lasted for more than an
hour. I formed my own opinion of the prisoner and I have had a
pretty wide experience of men. I thought him a very good type; a
born leader with really surprisingly little of the fanatic about him.

ARCHIBISHOP

Yes. I don't dispute that.

GOVERNOR

Moreover there is nothing in the indictment which calls for the death
penalty or anything like it. As far as I can see the man is guilty of nothing more than religious unorthodoxy. You can't kill him for that.

ARCHBISHOP

You are simply illustrating what I tried to refrain from saying about the importance which we attach to religion – and which you do not attach to it, whatever you may say. If you can't kill a man for religious unorthodoxy what can you kill him for?

GOVERNOR

My dear Archbishop –

ARCHBISHOP

I press the question. What can you kill him for?

GOVERNOR

Well, murder, I suppose, or incitement to revolt and violence. This fellow has been guilty of neither.

ARCHBISHOP

The objection to murder is fundamentally theological; God has not made us to deal arbitrarily with one another in matters of life and death. We object to revolt and sedition because we believe that God is not an anarchist, but that He wills law and order for His children. It is necessary to kill, if you must, in defence of these great concepts. But if you kill simply in support of your own opinion, or in defence of the political *status quo*, then you are a barbarian. I don't expect you to agree with me. You represent a way of life which is secular and over-civilized.

GOVERNOR

I see. Then we must agree to differ.

ARCHBISHOP

I have not come here to seek a theological or philosophical agreement. I have come with a death warrant which I must ask you to sign, since you represent the occupying power which denies to us the right to exercise capital punishment.

GOVERNOR

I am obliged to tell you that I shall not sign it. Your interpretation of your ecclesiastical duty as an obligation to take life is no concern of mine.

ARCHBISHOP

Then I shall have to state my case in terms that you will understand.

GOVERNOR

It is my duty to listen to you.

ARCHBISHOP

Let us look at the situation in this country calmly and objectively. We have a largely illiterate population with a small and powerful ruling-class. In that ruling class the Church has more influence than any other force. Therefore, he who controls the Church controls the country, virtually. You don't dispute that?

GOVERNOR

I don't think I should put it quite like that.

ARCHBISHOP

Then let us put it like this. In most countries of the world there is great agitation against the sort of occupation that you practise here. The colonial powers are everywhere on the retreat. No-one can doubt that in this country, too, there is a great popular desire for freedom. Yet there is no revolt and there is no threat of violence. Why is that?

GOVERNOR

You want me to say that it is because of the influence of the Church.

ARCHBISHOP

Never mind what I want you to say. What are the facts? I'll tell you. I have decided that my people are not ready as yet to govern themselves. I therefore remain on friendly terms with you, the occupying Power; the Church does as I say and the country does as the Church says. Is that true, or not? And I have decreed that our progress towards self-determination should be gradual and peaceful. Is *that* true or not?

GOVERNOR

It is certainly an explanation that covers most of the facts of the case.

ARCHBISHOP

Thank you. Now, supposing that I were replaced by someone else – that your people could no longer be sure that the voice of the Church, which is the voice of the nation, would be my voice. What then?

GOVERNOR

That is merely a speculation; how can I answer such a question? The answer depends on too many imponderables.

ARCHBISHOP

Speculation? Your Excellency, the possibility is far less remote than you seem to think. The followers of that agitator whom you interrogated an hour ago have a different conception of the Church from yours and mine. Never mind whether he's got political designs or not. He represents an idea that's dynamite. If his followers get the bit between their teeth I shan't be able to command the loyalty of the Church in six months, and you'll have a Cyprus on your hands in twelve. That's not speculation; it's cold, logical reasoning and anyone who knows the political situation here will tell you the same.

GOVERNOR

You must forgive me if I say that I think you're exaggerating the whole thing. You can't really believe that unless I agree to the execution of one obscure fanatic the whole situation will burst into flame.

ARCHBISHOP

Of course I do. That's how all revolutions come about – through the failure of people in authority to kill one fanatic at the right time.

GOVERNOR

But this is all guesswork; you haven't made out a capital case against the man or anything like it.

ARCHBISHOP *(sharply)*

Look. We're concerned with something far more urgent than what happens to one firebrand. Look at the international situation. If this fellow's supporters are allowed to turn me out you'll face an ultimatum within weeks; you'll be expected to hand over power to a lot of political morons or take the consequences, which will be armed rebellion. That's a situation that'ld please your enemies and harm your friends. Weapons and volunteers will be poured into the country by you know who; the United Nations will be split by intrigue and the ultimate world conflict may begin – as a result of it. The international situation is as delicately poised as that and you can't deny it. Beware how you allow anyone to dispute the equilibrium.

GOVERNOR

You must excuse my saying, your Grace, that I find a certain inconsistency in your complaints against this man. At the beginning of our discussion you conceded that he was guilty of nothing more than religious unorthodoxy and claimed that that was sufficient reason for executing him. Now you are saying that he may be the cause of a world war. Which is your real accusation?

ARCHBISHOP

Why should we play with words? I haven't altered my ground: I have merely expressed my case in terms which you can understand. I will state it again, simply. Here is a man who claims, or whose followers claim for him (it doesn't matter which) that he has an authority from God which sets him above me, the authentic representative of the Church. Owing to the climate of our times, which is perpetually favourable to anarchy, there is a very real danger that lawless elements will combine to enable him to prevail. If that happens you will be one stride away from a popular rising in the name of self-determination and perhaps two strides away from an international crisis of the gravest kind. All these consequences will be averted if you will sign this warrant and give me the right to turn my own bodyguard into a firing squad. There is no-one else in the country with the personality to do what this man can do. Your duty is clear. What is one man's life where these issues are concerned?

GOVERNOR

There is such a thing as justice, your Grace. This man has done nothing worthy of death.

ARCHBISHOP

Justice is a very good word and we shall have leisure to talk of it again when the crisis is over. But at the moment we are on the edge of disaster and the relevant vocabulary consists of only a few stern necessary words. Justice is not one of them. I have told you what are the consequences. To close your eyes to them is nothing more than sentimentality.

GOVERNOR

I have nothing to do with all these metaphors, Archbishop. I am a simple servant of my country and I must do my duty by the principles that I have learnt. I will not murder this man to save you from the dangers which threaten your Church. It is not my business to look beyond that decision to its consequences.

ARCHBISHOP

Very well. I have one more argument to put before you, of a more personal nature perhaps, and I think that you would prefer to discuss it alone.

GOVERNOR

As you please. Robert, will you . . .?

A.D.C.

Of course, sir.

[*He leaves the room.*]

GOVERNOR

What is this mysterious, personal reason, your Grace?

ARCHBISHOP

There is nothing mysterious about it. But young men are not often realists and Captain Cameron would no doubt have misunderstood what I am about to say. My dear Governor, you and I are both experienced, practical men and you will appreciate frankness, no doubt. What I want to say is that you can't afford to oppose me in this matter.

GOVERNOR

I don't understand you.

ARCHBISHOP

I will be brutally frank. It is essential to your political masters to preserve the tranquillity of this country. They have staked the whole of their colonial reputation on it, and you know as well as I do that failure in the colonial field would bring down the government in a matter of weeks. If you refuse to let me execute this man, I shall defend myself against him and his followers by taking a leaf out of their book. In other words, I shall bid for popularity here by making demands which your people cannot concede. And then we shall rebel and I shall be the popular hero of my people. It will be the only way left open to me. And I shall make it plain that it is you who have driven me to take this action.

GOVERNOR

This is blackmail.

ARCHBISHOP

I hope that you will reconsider that opinion. I am not making threats. I am only telling you what you will force me to do, if you deny me my request. You will force me to put into operation a chain of events which cannot fail to produce an armed rising here, with the consequent fall of your Government. At any rate, I think so; you will know if I am right. Beyond that the possible consequences are almost unimaginable – so great, indeed, that I will not insult you by suggesting that the end of your own diplomatic career will count for very much in your reckoning.

[*The Governor is silent, struggling with conflicting thoughts. After a few moments –*]

ARCHBISHOP

All this can be averted, if you will simply write your name at the bottom of this piece of paper. After all, I am not asking you to do very much – only to give permission for something which we ought to be allowed to do without permission. I will take full responsibility. [*He puts a document down on the desk. After a moment's silence the Governor picks up a pen.*]

GOVERNOR

All right. You really leave me no alternative. But you know what I think of the whole horrible business.

ARCHBISHOP (*consciously master of the situation*)

Yes, I know what you think. I have said that I accept full responsibility. (*The Governor signs the warrant and hands it to the other man.*) Thank you. The prisoner is in the cell below, I believe. My men are quite prepared. It won't take long. (*He moves to the door and then turns.*) I should like to congratulate you, if you won't misunderstand me, on your statesman-like decision. In such a context it takes a wise man to take the long view and it takes a courageous man to change his mind. You have done both and I admire you for it.

GOVERNOR

You have got your own way: that is what matters to you.

Let us leave out the compliments and do what has to be done. [*The Archbishop goes out and the Governor sits at the table for a moment with his head in his hands. He straightens up as the* A.D.C. *returns.*]

A.D.C.

Well, the old man was pretty sticky wasn't he, sir? I didn't think you'd get rid of him so soon. Did you manage to pacify him all right?

GOVERNOR (*grimly*)

Yes, he's pretty pacified, I think.

A.D.C. (*looking at him sharply*)

How do you mean, sir?

GOVERNOR

I mean that the Archbishop has gone away in a very contented frame of mind. He has no reason for complaint.

A.D.C.

Good God! You don't mean that he persuaded you to –

GOVERNOR

Robert, you will learn as you grow older that these things are rarely as simple or straightforward as they seem at first sight. (*He goes on, gaining strength, as if he were talking to convince himself rather than the other man.*) In our profession we are not often confronted with a simple choice between good and evil. Such choices are never difficult for a man who has been properly trained. The real issue is always between two evils or between two goods, to put it another way – between the lesser and the greater loyalty. It is such choices that test the character and fibre of a man and it is in such situations that he reveals whether or not he is capable of carrying the burdens of office; so it has been today. The situation which has arisen . . .

[*He breaks off as they hear the sound of heavy feet marching outside. A voice gives remote orders: 'Prisoner and escort – halt.' The party halts. There is the sound of three pairs of feet marching; then of two pairs of feet returning. A moment of silence, then 'Party – Fire!' There is a volley of shots. Then silence. The Governor stands facing the window, his back to the audience, rigidly at attention.*]

A.D.C.

Merciful God! Was that . . .

GOVERNOR (*swinging round*)

I took the hard decision. I did what I had to do. The responsibility for this man's death is not mine. History will know what to say about my conduct in this matter.

A.D.C. (*remotely, as if talking to himself*)

History will know what to say.

I believe in God the Father Almighty, Maker of Heaven and earth, and in Jesus Christ his only son our Lord, who was conceived by the Holy Ghost, born of the Virgin Mary, suffered under Pontius Pilate . . . (*The choir join in antiphonally*) . . . suffered under Pontius Pilate . . . suffered under Pontius Pilate . . . (*the* A.D.C. *facing Governor.*)

[*The Governor collapses into a chair and buries his face in his hands. The curtain slowly falls.*]

SERVICE FOR GOOD FRIDAY

CHOIR

'Were you there when they crucified my Lord?'

THE PREACHER (*reads*)

'When Pilate saw that he could prevail nothing but rather a tumult was made, he took water and washed his hands before the multitude saying "I am innocent of the blood of this just man: see ye to it."'

[*The lights are dimmed. A spotlight picks out a figure sitting on a stool and staring over the congregation.*]

PILATE

I am here, but not to justify myself.
I thought *I* was the judge, but judgment came
And I am *judged*. It has become my torment
That down the ages countless voices speak,
Merciless, certain and unanimous
'Suffered under Pontius Pilate'. I have heard them
Confident in their condemnation. People
Who never bore the weight of great decision,
Who never knew the fear that lives with power
Who did their sinning meanly, who were tempted
On an ignoble scale; whose cowardice
Was an affair of corners and of darkness;
These have all said their verdict, and have despised
My futile gesture, efforts to be neutral,
The silly basin, the pitiable washing of the hands,
Have left me in the ditch of my humiliation

And passed by on the other side.
I am not come to justify myself,
But this I say –
[*He stands.*]
If *you* have looked on evil and been neutral,
If you have watched the mob afflict the weak
And have not raised your voice in their defence;
If you have laughed at sneers and scorned the simple;
If you have seen unmoved the alien exploited
And tolerated the unspeakable vulgarity
With which men still afflict the Jew and Negro;
If in the small arena of your life
You have not taken sides;
If in the time of choice, the day of decision,
You have not dared to be different,
But have told the lie that everybody tells,
And have echoed like the sheep's bleat, the offensive idiom,
Have joined in the fashionable blasphemies,
Then this I will say;
Christ suffered under Pontius Pilate; true.
Does he not suffer – daily – under you?
[*The light fades and the Preacher reads again from the pulpit.*]

PREACHER

'And forthwith Judas came unto Jesus and he said, "Hail, Master",
and he kissed him.'
[*The spotlight picks out a second figure.*]

JUDAS

I know what you're thinking and I can't blame you. You're saying
to yourselves that it may be possible to make excuses for Pilate, but
that no-one can be expected to find anything to say for me. Yes,
that's right. I'm Judas. What could there be to say? The thing is so
appalling. I lived with Goodness and I sold it into the power of evil
for a handful of silver. You can't get lower than that. You can't
really imagine getting as low as that, can you? Well, can you?
I think perhaps you can. Let me explain. Why do you think I did it?

Do you think it was for the money? You can't really think that surely. Look what happened. I got the money all right, but when I saw what was happening I tried to get them to take it back, only of course they wouldn't. So I threw it away. Well, what good was it to me? I saw by then quite clearly what I had done. It was what people have now learnt to call a moment of truth and money isn't any good to you then. No, of course I didn't really do it for the money.

Money couldn't help when I knew that I had to go and hang myself. Why then? Because I hated him? Don't be silly. How could I hate him? No-one who knew him hated him. It wasn't possible. I did it because I loved him. It had to be that. The only people you ever want to kill are those whom you hate and those whom you love. You think that's absurd? Then you don't know much about life. Read some of the great literature of the world. Why did Othello kill Desdemona? Because he loved her so much. That's why Antony and Cleopatra destroyed each other. You can read the same thing on a less grand scale in the Sunday papers most weeks. Look into your own life. Those ideals that you hold, those ambitions that other people have for you, those visions and dreams that visit you at your best moments and make such demands on you – don't you love them, and don't you shirk them and don't you destroy them? Of course you do. In a moment of fury you go ahead and destroy them. That's what was wrong with me. I had to be like him and to follow him wherever he led, whatever it meant, or I had to kill him. The poets know all about it.

And each man kills the thing he loves,
   By each let this be heard.
Some do it with a bitter look,
   Some with a flattering word.
The coward does it with a kiss,
   The brave man with a sword.

I was a coward, there's no doubt about that, so I did it with a kiss.

Some people do it in a more dignified way, but most people do it, don't they? I mean it simply isn't true that I stand by myself on a lonely pinnacle of infamy. You don't need to look very deep to find one within you.

[*The light fades and the Preacher reads again.*]

PREACHER

'Then Peter denied with an oath, saying I do not know the man . . . And he went out and wept bitterly.'

[*A figure comes down the aisle from the back and climbs into the pulpit.*]

PETER

I'd like to tell you about that. I'm Peter. I've come into the pulpit because I'm going to preach to you. Not for long, you've had the first two headings of the sermon and mine is the last.

That was a very cowardly performance of mine, I know, and I'm still ashamed of it, though I was fully and generously forgiven. Why do you think that the Church told the story from the earliest days and put it down in the written gospel? It would have been better propaganda wouldn't it to suppress the story? After all, I was one of the two main leaders in the new Church, and you'd think that it was important for the people, both Christian and anti-Christian, to think highly of me. It's like finding a religious newspaper telling stories about the shortcomings of one of the Archbishops.

We told this story as a warning, because the way in which I treated Jesus is the way in which we all treat him. I was such an enthusiast. I was the first person to recognize who he was, and when I blurted out, 'You are the Christ, the Son of God,' he was very pleased with me. Later I was over-confident and I said all sorts of extravagant things about dying for him, and when he warned me of the way in which I was going to behave I thought that he must be mad. I had to find out the hard way that enthusiasm and idealism are all very well in their way, but there's no substitute for stamina. There I was quite alone; there were no other Christians to see my enthusiasm or to stiffen my backbone. And he'd just been arrested without any resistance. The whole of our cause seemed to have collapsed and I was left to face cold facts and a circle of hostile faces. That's how it happened.

What would you have done? Before you answer too confidently, let me say this. This is a country with a Christian tradition. There are thousands of people in it who have committed themselves publicly to a Christian allegiance. They have promised to follow Christ; they have openly joined his Church, and they have known that what was demanded of them was not only enthusiasm, but also discipline and obedience. Where are they when the church bells ring? Where are they when the Last Supper is remembered at an inconvenient, uncomfortable hour? They face, not persecutions, scarcely even ridicule, but loss of comfort, and they are not there. I am here to remind you in all charity that there are many ways of denying Christ.

Prayers – followed by 'When I survey the Wondrous Cross'.
Benediction.

EVERYMAN

COMMENTATOR

Five hundred years ago, or so, before drama became sophisticated, when everyone believed that the teaching of the Church was true, most plays were religious in their themes. They used to act a play called Everyman. Everyman was the ordinary man – you or I, the man the BBC interviews in the street or the woman in the ITV advertisement; the statistic in the Public Opinion Polls. This is a story about 20th-century Everyman. I'm the Commentator. In the old play they might have called me the Angel and that's what I really am. Not *your* idea of an Angel, perhaps: come to think of it, what *is* your idea of an Angel? Of course you're not superstitious nowadays so you don't believe in Angels – only in Astrology and Advertisements and the Great God Luck.

What you are about to see is an episode in the life of Mr Everyman, a well-to-do member of the upper-middle class in this day and age, as they call it. I hope you'll find it interesting. Mr Everyman is in conversation with the Vicar. They are in Mr Everyman's office: the conversation has been going on for some time, and it is not going well for the Vicar.

VICAR

But surely you must agree that it is a good cause that I am pleading for?

EVERYMAN (*drily*)

Admirable, no doubt. That has nothing to do with my attitude.

VICAR

I know that you don't belong to my Church and that you have no sympathy with what it stands for. If I were appealing for some religious activity I should understand your position. I could have no possible claim on you. But this has nothing to do with the Church. The Old People's Home for which I am trying to raise money will cater for people in need, whether they are Church people or not. Most of them won't be. The need is desperate: otherwise . . .

EVERYMAN

Otherwise you would not have come to me. I quite understand. I am a notoriously difficult man to extract money from.

VICAR (*whose patience is wearing thin*)

As you say.

EVERYMAN

It's as well that we should understand each other. I could give you five thousand pounds without feeling it. But I do not propose to do so. I should like to tell you why. You've earned an explanation by your courage in undertaking the uncongenial task of approaching me.

VICAR

I have no right to ask for an explanation. But I confess that I am curious to hear your point of view.

EVERYMAN

Then here it is. I have two reasons for refusing your request; one is practical; the other you might call principle. The practical reason is very simple. If I said Yes to you, I should be giving the green light to a flood of do-gooders, who would tread each other down in the rush to bleed me white, in aid of their pet charities. You must agree that that is probable.

VICAR

Of course. But it would still be in your power to exercise discrimination and responsibility in the management of your great wealth.

EVERYMAN

I've quite enough to do without that. But my second reason is more important. I have called it a matter of principle, and a man of your calling has surely a respect for principles.

VICAR

For some more than for others.

EVERYMAN

No doubt. My principle is based on a hatred of charity. (*The Vicar lifts his hand in protest and starts to speak but Everyman holds up his hand and talks him down.*)

VICAR

But surely . . .

EVERYMAN

Vicar, twice every Sunday you stand in your pulpit and expound your creed and no-one is allowed to interrupt you. Now you are in the pew and I'm in the pulpit. Be good enough to allow me to preach my sermon without interruption. It will be far shorter than yours; and – as I've already indicated – it will not be followed by a collection.

[*The Vicar inclines his head gravely and remains silent.*]

I have said that I hate charity. I hate it because it denies everything that I believe in. My father started life as a poor man and he died a millionaire. Every penny that he owned he made by his own efforts. When I went away to school at the age of 13 he said, 'they'll teach you to stand on your own feet and that's all you need to learn from *them*. Life is a struggle; every man for himself!' That's what he said and the old man was dead right. All my life I've proved it. Of course there are people who can't take it and they come to grief. It's the job of the state to look after them. We've got a Welfare State to do just that. I pay my taxes without grumbling and a lot of what I pay is used to prop up the failures and make life easier for them. Well, that's all I'm paying.

VICAR

And that is what you call your principle?

EVERYMAN

Yes, by God it is! And it's most people's principle, only most haven't the guts to say so. Your religion's had a long run, Vicar, but it's on the way out now. The Good Samaritan has had his day. There is no help in God and no help in man. The only help is to help yourself. That's my religion and you'll find that – unlike most religious people – I practise what I preach.

VICAR (*rising*)

I see. It remains only for me to thank you for receiving me and to express the hope that life will treat you better than your creed deserves.

EVERYMAN (*casually*)

I ask no better treatment. Good day.

[*Exeunt.*]

[*The Angel rises and addresses the audience conversationally.*]

COMMENTATOR

What do you think of that? A bit improbable, do you think, to get a man talking in that way? Perhaps you're right. But you'd agree, wouldn't you, that a lot of people *think* in that way, and one of the conventions of drama is to show people saying what they really think – like the soliloquies in 'Hamlet'. I'm supposed to be the commentator, so I'd better make a comment on that scene. Here it is. 'Whatsoever a man soweth, that shall he also reap.' A square remark, I'm afraid. But then, in some ways, it's a square world. Mr Everyman had a bit of bad luck when he left the office that evening. He and his Jaguar ran into a neat little ambush. It was quite simple. He saw the light of a torch in the middle of the road and behind it a man in an official-looking hat signalling to him to stop. So he came to a halt and put his head out of the window to find out what was happening. That was what the man wanted him to do. It made it possible for him to hit him over the head and take all his money, as well as his car. We're not showing you the scene; partly because it's easier not to have to put a Jaguar on the stage and partly because violence in drama always makes people laugh; you see so much of it on television. It wasn't very funny for Mr Everyman and I don't want you to laugh at him. As a matter of fact they left him in rather bad shape. He's a bit concussed, so he may not be seeing things very clearly.

[*Everyman enters and sits on the ground.*]

COMMENTATOR

By chance a certain pedestrian came where he was.

[*An ordinary man enters.*]

EVERYMAN (*feebly*)

Help me!

ORDINARY MAN

Hullo, what's this? Good Heavens, you *are* in a bad way, old chap. What happened? Hit and run driver? (*He keeps his distance.*)

EVERYMAN

I've been attacked and robbed. Get me a doctor.

ORDINARY MAN

Attacked, eh? *And* robbed? Look here, I don't want to get involved in anything. The police are bound to be along in a moment. Better leave it to them.

EVERYMAN (*desperately*)

Can't you ring an ambulance, or something? You can't leave me. No-one may come for hours.

ORDINARY MAN

Awfully sorry, old chap. I'd like to help, but I'm on my way to an appointment and I mustn't be late. To be honest with you, I can't stand the sight of blood. I've always been funny like that. And I don't want to get mixed up in anything nasty, if you see what I mean. You'll be all right; someone will come along. After all this is a civilized country in the 20th century . . . (*This last sentence is something that he gabbles reassuringly as he hurries out and we hear his voice fading away in the distance.*)

[*Everyman falls back despairingly and calls feebly for help once or twice.*]

COMMENTATOR

By chance a certain physician came where he was. (*Enter Dr Luke.*)

EVERYMAN

Who's that? Help!

DR LUKE

Mr Everyman? What are you doing here?

EVERYMAN

Dr Luke? Thank God you've come. What a stroke of luck that my own doctor should turn up just when I need him.

DR LUKE

It's entirely by chance, I assure you. Is there something that you want?

EVERYMAN

Something that I want? What sort of question's that? Can't you see I've been knocked about like the devil? Get me to a hospital! I'm bleeding to death.

DR LUKE

I shouldn't think so. Your wound looks very superficial from here. But you can hardly expect a thorough medical examination from me at this time of night. I'm not on duty now. I've had a very long day and I'm entitled, like any other man, to a little leisure at the end of it. I bid you good night.

EVERYMAN

Good Heavens, what sort of doctor do you call yourself?

DR LUKE

You have surprisingly romantic notions of my profession for a realist, sir. Perhaps you are confusing me with Dr Kildare or Dr Finlay. I prescribe for you a little less television and a little more study of the true nature of life as we know it.

[*He strides off angrily. Everyman falls back with a groan.*]

COMMENTATOR

By chance a certain priest came where he was.

[*Enter the Vicar.*]

EVERYMAN (*hardly daring to believe it*)

Is that really you, Vicar?

VICAR

Yes, it is. Is there something that you want to say to me?

EVERYMAN (*hysterically*)

I should rather think that there is. I have been waylaid and beaten up, robbed and left here to die, and no-one will do anything for me. A man came along who looked like an ordinary decent chap, but he wouldn't lift a finger to help. And then my own doctor turned up, but he wouldn't behave like a doctor. He said he wasn't on duty and pushed off. Thank God you've come. Now I shall be all right.

VICAR

Indeed? May I ask when you last visited my Church?

EVERYMAN

Not for years I'm afraid. But surely that doesn't matter.

VICAR

A very odd belief. There are thousands like you on the earth. They like to have a Church to make use of when they need it – when someone dies, for instance – but they won't move a muscle to keep it there when they think they can get on without it. Well, that's all finished with.

EVERYMAN

What do you mean? *You* can't be refusing your help.

VICAR

'There is no help in God and no help in man. The only help is to help yourself.' Do you remember saying that?

EVERYMAN

You're not going to hold that against me, are you?

VICAR

It's nothing to do with me. It's the rule of this place that everyone must abide by his own creed.

EVERYMAN

This place? What do you mean?

VICAR

You must try to understand. Don't you know that you are dead and this place is Hell?

[*Everyman reels back in a faint and the curtain is closed.*]

COMMENTATOR

Of course, it didn't really happen like that. I told you the man was concussed and what you have seen was his dream. The first person who found him called an ambulance. His doctor rushed round to see him at once. I believe that the Vicar called on him and brought him some grapes. But he did a bit of thinking during his convalescence and he'd like to read you his favourite bit of the Bible.

[*Everyman enters and reads the parable of the Good Samaritan. (St Luke X, 25–37).*]
Prayer.
Hymn.
Benediction.
Nunc Dimittis.

There should be no dressing up (except that the Vicar can wear a clerical collar). The actors get up and come forward from their places in the congregation when they are due on the 'stage'.

The whole 'production' is impressionistic; the original Everyman should be borne in mind. There is very little distinction, if any, between the actors and the audience.

The whole point of the play, of course, is the reading of the parable at the end. It ought to be read as well as possible – *I* think, from the Authorized Version.

DANIEL À LA KOSSOFF
STORIES FOR WEEKDAY MORNING PRAYERS

Monday

The Book of Daniel is an extraordinary book. You ought to read it. It is full of the most remarkable happenings, but nothing is as remarkable as the people who appear in it. And the most remarkable was Daniel. He could have been an outstanding man in any company. I'll tell you about him.

To begin with he was an extraordinarily courageous person. He had simple values and beliefs and nothing that happened to him could make him believe any differently from the way in which he thought that he ought to believe. When he was only a child his country was conquered and overrun by the Babylonians and he was one of a number of boys who were carried in captivity to the King's Court. Nebuchadnezzar was the King. He was a great, stupid, ignorant creature who had always had his own way; like a spoilt child he thought that he always would. He was very much mistaken. Daniel showed no less courage early on. It was a matter of religious practice with him to be very careful about what he ate and drank. Now the King had put a man in charge of the young prisoners and told him that they were to be given all sorts of special food and drink so that they might become strong healthy boys. When Daniel stuck in his toes these men told him to get on with it and eat what he was given without arguing. But this remarkable boy made up his mind that he and his companions would be true to their principles – and nothing that the Babylonians could say would shake him. And he told the men that in ten days they would prove that they were fitter than the children who lived on the official diet. And so they did.

He was a very strong-minded child and no-one could budge him from this course once he had made up his mind that it was right. That's why he grew up into the sort of man that he became.

Daniel wasn't only brave. He was something that is even rarer, he was very intelligent. When he grew up he was regarded as one of the wisest men in the Kingdom. Nebuchadnezzar was a silly superstitious sort of man. When he had dreams and visions he asked his army of astrologers what they meant and they had to admit that they hadn't a clue. So the spoilt child on the throne was furious and he actually made a decree that all the wise men were to be killed. And most of them were killed, but they weren't really wise so they were no great loss. But when they came to kill Daniel he said, 'Wouldn't it be better if I told the King the meaning of the things that puzzle him?' So he told the King what he wanted to know (for God had revealed it to him) and the King was wild with delight and promoted Daniel to be chief wise man in place of all the ones that he had eliminated. And he said that he would worship Daniel's God. So everything should have been all right. But it wasn't because, as I told you, Nebuchadnezzar was a very silly man. You'll see tomorrow what he did.

Tuesday

I told you yesterday about Daniel's wisdom and how he interpreted the King's dreams. The King was so pleased with him that he made him ruler over the whole province of Babylon, and when Daniel asked him to appoint three friends of his, men of the same type as himself, to the chief positions of influence under him, the King agreed at once. You'll have heard of them. They were called Shadrach, Meshach and Abednego. I want to remind you of the astonishing story in which they were concerned.

Nebuchadnezzar was one of the greatest Kings that the world had ever seen and he was also one of the stupidest men that ever drew breath. After quite a short time he forgot all about worshipping Daniel's God, which was what he had promised to do, and he decided to put on a great demonstration of his own power. He had a colossal statue made all of gold, one of the most vulgar status symbols of all time. He had it placed in a vast open space called the Plain of Dura, in the province of Babylon, where Daniel's three friends were the most prominent and influential people. Then he called together into the plain an enormous assembly including all the top people – judges, governors, captains, counsellors – the lot. When they were all assembled, wondering what on earth the royal mountebank was up to now, a herald with a terrific voice made this announcement: 'You see the statue that the King has set up? By royal decree that is now your god. In a moment you will hear the sound of music from the greatest collection of instruments in the world. That is the signal. Everyone is to bow down and worship the statue. Long live Nebuchadnezzar.' Then he added something. 'Anyone who disobeys,' he said 'will be burnt alive.'

There was a deep silence while the message sank in. And then the silence was broken by a tremendous crash of music.

Nebuchadnezzar may have been a stupid man, but no-one underestimated his power. This was a supremely silly decree in a very silly career, but no-one laughed. If you had been present in the plain of Dura that day you would have seen a most impressive spectacle. It was like the wind passing over a cornfield. As the music died away that vast crowd of distinguished and important people swayed forward and bowed down in front of that grotesque idol, as one man. No, not quite as one man. In spite of the almost invisible pull of mob behaviour, three men remained on their feet, like guardsmen on parade – Shadrach, Meshach and Abednego, Daniel's officers, and men after his own heart. It was a very impressive display of courage and character; you'll see what it led to tomorrow.

Wednesday

As you can imagine, there were a good many Babylonians who had always resented the promotion of three Jews to the chief positions in the province. Now they saw their chance. They went to the King and said, 'You know those three foreigners you put in charge of the province? We warned you about them. It seems we were right.' Nebuchadnezzar rounded on them indignantly. 'Are you getting at

Shadrach, Meshach and Abednego again?' he said. 'Now once and for all . . .' One of the Babylonians, more brave than the others, had the temerity to interrupt. 'O King, live for ever,' he said, automatically, 'I thought you might like to know that they refused to bow down and worship your statue. Everyone saw them remain on their feet when the music sounded. There's been a good deal of talk.'

To say that the King was furious means nothing. He had the three Jews dragged into his presence and stormed at them for about half an hour. In the end he said, 'Now, listen to me. I'll give you one more chance. You can go back into that plain and worship my image, or you can go into my furnace. It's very hot and I shall see that it is made hotter. I can assure you that there is no God that will be able to deliver you out of my hand.'

The three men looked at one another as if deciding silently which was to be the spokesman. Two of them nodded quietly and the third spoke, with indescribable calm and confidence. 'There's no problem in answering that, your Majesty,' he said. 'The God whom we all serve *can* deliver us and He *will* deliver us. But even if He doesn't, we shall not bow down and worship that idol. There isn't any question of that.' The other two nodded again and silence fell, broken only by the sound of an absolute tyrant fighting for breath.

Then the storm broke. Nebuchadnezzar raved like a lunatic. He had more and more fuel piled on the furnace until the heat was so great that it killed the stokers. Then he had the three men bound hand and foot, and flung into the heart of the furnace. Then he sat back and watched.

A few moments later, shaking with fear, he grabbed the arm of his nearest counsellor. 'How many men did we throw into the flames?' he asked. 'Three, your Majesty.' 'Bound hand and foot?' 'Yes, your Majesty.' 'Look,' he said, pointing a trembling finger, 'there are four men there, and free, and the fourth one looks like a Son of God.'

You can guess the rest. This extraordinary potentate did exactly what he had done before. He announced to the whole nation that Shadrach, Meshach and Abednego were restored to the highest position in the land, that their God was the only true God and that anyone who failed to worship him would be cut to pieces. He was, of course, a kind of lunatic, like many very powerful and successful men. It is always necessary that there should be found men with the courage and faith to stand up against that kind of lunacy.

Tomorrow we go back to Daniel.

Thursday

When Nebuchadnezzar, the great King of Babylon, died he was succeeded by his son, Belshazzar, who seems to have been just the sort of son that you would expect Nebuchadnezzar to have. He forgot all about the God whom his father had learnt to worship and he forgot all about Daniel, whom his father had promoted above all the wise men in the Kingdom. He gave himself up to a life of self-indulgence and luxury. He turned his back on duty and obligation and lived like a pampered animal, deaf to all advice and warning. The end came very suddenly, as it often does to such people.

One night he held an enormous feast, attended by a thousand guests. It was an orgy of food and drink, especially drink, and he added sacrilege to his other enormities, by taking the vessels which had been stolen from the temple in Jerusalem and using them as cups for his banquet. When the fun was at its height, a very sobering thing happened; at any rate it sobered the King and his guests all right, and that took a bit of doing. The figure of a man's hand, it seemed, appeared suddenly and wrote on the wall of the palace four words in an unknown tongue, and then the fingers vanished as mysteriously as they had come.

The King was terrified. Like everyone else, he had a conscience. If this supernatural message had anything to do with his deserts he knew that it could have no good meaning. Not to understand it was intolerable. He sought for all the wise men and astrologers, who had shot up like weeds since the liquidation of a generation ago, and promised them tremendous rewards if they would interpret the writing, but they were either unable or afraid to do so. And the King grew sick with panic. Then his wife reminded him of Daniel, whose wisdom had stood his father in good stead, and who now lived forgotten and in obscurity. So the King sent for Daniel and promised him great gifts and a high position if he could interpret the writing. Daniel said, 'You can keep your gifts, O King. It is my *job* to tell you the truth as God reveals it to me.' He read the message on the wall and then he faced the King fearlessly.

'You have forgotten God,' he said. 'Your father learned through bitter experience to honour and worship Him, but you have ignored everything that he learned. You have given up yourself to luxury and idolatry. And now God sends you this message. It says that the period of your rule is over. You have been weighed in the scales and found wanting. Your kingdom is to be taken from you and given to the Medes and the Persians.'

Belshazzar was still capable of recognizing the truth when he heard it. He gave orders that a golden chain should be given to Daniel and that he should be made the third ruler in the kingdom. But he never gave any more orders. That very night he met his end in battle and the Babylonian empire fell into the hand of Darius the Persian, just as Daniel had said.

Friday

The new King, Darius the Persian, recognized the quality of Daniel at once. He was a good judge of men and Daniel's character stuck out a mile. He appointed a hundred and twenty princes to rule over the Kingdom, and three presidents to supervise the princes and he made Daniel senior president. The other rulers were madly jealous of the Jew who had been put over them and it wasn't long before they combined against him. They were ingenious men and they produced a very neat little plot.

They knew that there were no flaws in Daniel's character and that if they were to hit at him it must be through his religion. So they went to the King and flattered him outrageously. And then one of them said, 'It is essential that these conquered people should recognize your supremacy, O King. So we suggest that you make a rule that, for the next month, anyone found offering worship to any God or man, other than yourself, should be thrown into a den of lions. And if you will sign the decree, O King, it will make it one of the laws of the Medes and

Persians, that never alter.' The King walked straight into the trap and signed the decree. Then the plotters watched Daniel to see how he would meet the problem.

Daniel saw no problem. It was his invariable custom to open a window of his house facing Jerusalem, three times a day, and pray to God, and he had no hesitation at all in continuing the practice. His enemies, in high triumph, went to the King and made their report. Darius was acutely embarrassed. 'O well,' he said, 'Daniel's a little different. I didn't mean it to apply . . .' 'But your majesty,' said the spokesman, 'your decree made no exceptions. Look, here is your signature, and that makes it a law of the Medes and Persians which never alter.' And Darius saw that he was trapped. He spent a whole day trying to find a way out, but of course there wasn't one.

Darius was very apologetic to Daniel about it. 'But I have to enforce the decree,' he said. 'No doubt your God will protect you. You'll be all right, I hope.' Daniel said nothing and they fastened him securely in the lions' den.

The King had a dreadful night. He tossed sleeplessly on his bed, and very early in the morning he rushed to the lions' den and called out anxiously, 'Are you all right, Daniel?' There was a slight pause and his heart was in his mouth, and then he heard the calm, reassuring voice of his victim. 'It's all right,' said Daniel, 'God has stopped the mouths of the lions.' And when they opened the den he stepped out unhurt.

It wasn't that there was anything wrong with the lions. The plotters found that, when they discovered that it doesn't pay to set traps for tyrants. For Darius was so angry that he commanded them to be thrown into the den and when they begged for mercy he only said, 'I have decreed this according to the laws of the Medes and Persians, which never alter.' So that was the end of them.

Then Darius, like his predecessors before him, said that everyone must worship the God of Daniel, for He was the only great and loving God, and Daniel had proved it.

The point of all those stories in Daniel is that even hundreds of years ago men knew that the qualities of faith and courage were what give integrity and consistency to character. They still are.

TWO PARABLES

(a) The Recording Angel

It was a warm, drowsy afternoon in late June that Philipson had his first conversation with the Angel. He was feeling dissatisfied with life in general. He had just had a rather stormy interview with his House-master and he had retired to the bank on the cricket field to brood over his hard lot. The others who had been there during the earlier part of the afternoon had drifted away, most of them to the Baths, but Philipson lay lazily in the heat of the sun, watching the school bats-men dealing with some not very formidable bowling and experiencing that delicious sense of vacancy which a hot summer afternoon so easily induces. And suddenly he was aware of a man sitting on the grass beside him. He didn't know how he had got there and it didn't seem to matter. The visitor had a friendly look and Philipson found himself talking to him in a strange way. It was more like a continuation of his thoughts than starting a conversation.

'I suppose I was behaving rather badly in Chapel,' he said, 'but I don't know why he had to be so violent about it. Lots of other people do it.'

'I don't see what that's got to do with it,' said the Angel. 'Perhaps he thinks that you're capable of behaving better. Rather a compliment, really.'

'Don't you think they rather overdo this Chapel business here?' said Philipson. 'You look an understanding sort of chap. It's a bit hard to get anything out of it, especially in this hot weather.'

'Well I suppose that it depends a bit on how much you put into it, doesn't it?' answered the Angel.

129

Philipson kicked the ground angrily. 'That's the sort of thing they always say,' he said. 'I hoped for something better than that from you. What does it mean? How can you put anything into it? You can have a bash at the hymns if you like singing, but the rest of the time someone's reading at you or praying at you or preaching at you. How can you put anything into that?'

The Angel smiled at him in a very friendly way. 'You can concentrate,' he said. 'That's very hard work, I know, and people find it much easier not to do it. But you can't get anything worth while without it. What subjects are you going to do in the Sixth Form?'

'History and English,' said Philipson, 'and probably French, though I'd like to do Maths if I could. Why? What's that got to do with it?'

'It's got this to do with it,' said the Angel. 'You know quite well that it's harder work to read a History book or a play by Shakespeare than a paperback thriller from a bookstall. But you get far more out of it – if you put the effort into it. And how could you get the satisfaction that some people get out of Maths without concentrating? Are you fond of music?'

'Yes, very,' said Philipson.

'Then you know what I'm talking about. Anyone can give an easy superficial response to superficial music, but the good stuff makes demands on you if you're going to enjoy it. And the great stuff makes great demands. Why should you expect religion to be any easier? People give up religion and say that they can't get anything out of it who'd never dream of giving up reading good books or listening to good music after making such feeble efforts to appreciate them.'

'How do you know?' asked Philipson.

The Angel laughed. 'This is our biggest problem,' he said. 'You'd be surprised how early on in the service lots of people simply give up. And then they blame the preacher.'

'I don't see how you can be so sure,' said Philipson.

'Then I'll tell you,' said the Angel. 'You ought to hear our recordings. You've heard of the Recording Angel, of course. We have a department which records the thoughts that are really going through people's minds during a service, while they are apparently singing hymns and saying prayers. It's amazing how quickly some of them let their minds wander. I was listening the other day to a recording of a man during a hymn. It went something like this:

O God, our help in ages past,
Our hope for years to come,
How long's the sermon going to last,
    And when can I go home?

And in the general Confession, when he had got as far as 'We have erred and strayed from Thy ways like lost sheep' the tape registered a complete switch away from the prayer and he went on, 'Though I don't think I'm worse than anyone else; in fact I'm a good deal better than most.' From then on he was reminding himself of all his virtues and the General Confession finished as a Personal Congratulation.

Philipson nodded. 'I must admit all that sounds pretty true,' he said. 'Then what you mean is that we can't get anything out of religion without concentrating and that lots of people give up going to Church, not because there's something wrong with Christianity, but because they never give their minds to it?'

'That's right,' said the Angel.

There was a sharp click from the middle of the field and Philipson looked up to see the wicket-keeper picking up a bail and a figure setting off on the long walk back to the pavilion.

'He's out,' he said, 'and only eight runs short of his hundred. What rotten luck. What happened?'

'He lifted his head,' said the Angel, 'and hit over a yorker. I think his concentration must have gone. But I expect he knows what happened and whose fault it was. I don't think he'll blame the game, or give it up.'

Philipson sat up and rubbed his eyes. The shadows had lengthened across the ground, the players had gone their ways, the pitch was deserted and he was alone.

(b) The first step

'To thine own self be true.'

For some time Philipson had been feeling depressed about himself. It seemed to him sometimes that he was really two different people. When he was by himself he was full of the desire to display all the qualities that he really admired; he saw himself as hard-working and honest and kind to other people. But when he was with a crowd of his friends, which he enjoyed very much since he was a sociable person by nature, it seemed to him that his whole character altered. He liked to think of himself as a leader, but he knew somewhere in the back of his mind that really he followed the mood of the crowd. He recognized with dismay that popularity mattered to him more than anything else and that, in order to be in the swim, he was willing to be slack and not very scrupulous, that he was prepared to say and do almost anything for a laugh, and that he was capable, even of being cruel to other people who were out of favour. He wasn't especially introspective, but he had his moments of self-examination like the rest of us, and he wasn't very pleased with what he saw.

Things had come to a head that morning. It was a Sunday and he had listened to a rather good sermon (by a visiting preacher, of course) in which the congregation had been urged to be true to their real selves. At first he had felt uplifted and inspired, but after some thought he found himself in the grip of a black mood of depression. 'How do I know which is my real self?' he asked himself gloomily. 'For all I know it is this popular sort of buffoon that I seem to become in a crowd.' And the devil, who is always on hand when we are feeling depressed, cordially agreed with him. 'I expect that that is your real self,' whispered the devil. 'After all you spend most of your time being that self, don't you? Why not admit it?'

Philipson closed his eyes in agony, and when he opened them again there was his friend the Angel, looking as if he had been there all along. 'Did you hear what that devil said?' asked Philipson, urgently. And when the Angel nodded his head, he asked eagerly 'Is it true?'

'You mustn't bother about that,' said the Angel. 'Of course it isn't true.'

'I wish you'd prove that to me,' said Philipson, unhappily. 'Well, I can't prove it,' said the Angel, 'but I can give you plenty of evidence, and I'll give it you very quickly, because you've had one sermon this morning already, and you don't want another. First of all, if you want to understand about your true self you must understand who made you and what you were made for. After all, that's only common sense. If you saw an old Rolls-Royce rusting away in the middle of a farmyard, with poultry clambering all over it, you'd feel sorry. You'd know that it was made by a great engineer and that he designed it to carry people about and you'd feel sorry that it had degenerated into a sort of hen-coop.'

'Yes,' said Philipson. 'That's all right about a Rolls. But how do I know that it's true about me?'

'Because you want it to be true,' answered the Angel promptly. 'That's the real evidence. If your nature were really that of a kind of moral hen-coop you'd be quite happy to be your worse self, instead of longing to be your better self. The Christian religion is all about that, and that's all it *is* about really. The people who followed Jesus followed him because he showed them what they could be like – Matthew the traitor, Zacchaeus, the cheat, and Peter, the liar and coward. If you weren't bothered about yourself you'd make a very good Pharisee, but a very poor Christian. The fact that you're fed-up with yourself means that you've taken the first step in religion – and a very big step too.'
'What's the next one?' asked Philipson, who was beginning to feel a little less gloomy.

'Look it up,' said the Angel. 'It'll do you good to do a bit of work for a change. The answer is in Matthew, chapter four, verse nineteen.'

That was all that Philipson got out of the Angel. In fact, having repeated the reference the Angel vanished and Philipson went off to look for his Bible. If you're interested in the story, you'd better do the same.

Matthew IV, 19.

Papers

CHRISTIAN EDUCATION

Education is, for many listeners no doubt, a forbidding theme, but thoughtful people who are concerned about the sort of world into which their children are growing up cannot help being interested in education. It is to such people that I am talking this afternoon. There is a good deal in the modern environment about which we are bound to be concerned. On the academic level there is scientific materialism, which is particularly dangerous to those who are pursuing scientific studies almost exclusively and to those who have not pursued them very thoroughly. On the social level there is a notorious decline in standards and an appalling problem in adolescent behaviour. On the political level there is a persistent challenge to the whole fabric of democracy. What has education to say in response to the urgent problems of our age? You may like to know the answer of one working schoolmaster.

If you read the works of writers about education in the past you will find that every one of them, from Plato to Thomas Arnold, succeeds in conveying a sense of purpose and a confidence of aim which are notably absent from modern writing. As we read their books we are impressed by the clarity with which they saw their goal. Dr Arnold, for instance, said that his aim at Rugby was to produce Christian gentlemen. You may not like the phrase: you may be agnostic about the adjective and contemptuous of the noun, but at least you must agree that there is something clear-cut about the educational objective described.

We don't talk like that today. Whether it is because we have broadened our outlook, or because we have lost our confidence, we prefer nowadays to seek refuge in woolly language which provides at best an ambiguous definition of aims.

'Education for life', 'Education for freedom', 'Education for Citizenship' – these are the sort of slogans with which modern educational writing is littered and the flabby abstract nouns tell their own tale of a purpose which has been lost. Dr Arnold could have told you in a few words what he meant by a Christian gentleman, but what clear educational aim emerges, in the mottoes which I have quoted from the words 'life', 'citizenship' and 'democracy'? The problem is not, of course, merely or mainly educational. Education does not proceed in a vacuum: it reflects, either by conforming with them or by reacting against them the values of the society in which it is carried out. Under a totalitarian regime the objective of education can be clearly stated. A Nazi schoolmaster said to me once, 'The difference between your schools and ours is that you wish your boys to think and we wish ours to know certain things.' It is easy for us to say, defensively, that Dr Arnold, and indeed Plato, were able to define their educational objective so clearly because, like the Nazi, they had a limited vision of the purpose of education. We claim that we have chosen the hard path of liberty and we must not, therefore, be asked to confine our aims within the rigid limits of definition. It is surely time for us to call a halt to this pretentious vagueness. It is a good thing to widen and lengthen the range of our vision, but only in order that we may concentrate on something which is further away. The man who sees everything sees nothing. If we are to avoid an objective which is bad, then we must choose an objective which is good, not seek refuge in one which is so vague that no-one can say whether it is bad or good. The abstract aims to which I have referred tell us nothing until we have answered the further questions they raise: 'Education for life' begs the question of 'what sort of life?': 'Education for freedom' the question of 'freedom to do what?': and 'Education for citizenship' the question of 'what sort of citizens?'. Let me repeat, Plato knew what he meant by the good life, and Arnold knew what he meant by Christian gentlemen: do we know what we mean? And let me add, to make the question more urgent, that Stalin knows what he means.

138

This question must be put, not only to educationists, but to the society which they represent. It is, of course, a religious question, because it demands of society a statement of its fundamental beliefs. My time is limited and I must say quite briefly what I believe to be the basic cause of our educational and social confusion. It arises from the fact that we have abandoned our belief in the Christian faith and its historic values; that we never had any good grounds for that abandonment: and that we have failed and are bound to fail to find any agreed standards to take the place of Christian standards.

There stands between Dr Arnold's time and our own the tragic controversy between Religion and Science, which did more than anything else to produce the modern vacuum of values. It is easy to see now that in that battle the greatest disservice that the champions of both sides could do to their cause was to admit that there was anything to fight about. But thousands of people today believe that somehow the historic faith, in which our civilization is rooted, was discredited about a hundred years ago by a man called Darwin, and they have abandoned a religion about which they know little at the behest of a science of which they know probably less. We live in a scientific age and on balance that is a matter for rejoicing, and not for regret. It is right that we should educate people in an understanding of the scientific climate of our times, but one of the dangers of a scientific education is that it has nothing to tell us of the spiritual values by which men live, and if it is pursued exclusively it can actually make us less qualified to pursue those values. There is a kind of scientific materialism which is one of the peculiar dangers of our age. We may become so satisfied with weighing and measuring those things which can be weighed and measured that we lose interest in the great imponderables and close our minds to the whole area of truth which lies outside the laboratory. Only a recovery of religion can rescue us from that danger. This is clearly a challenge – some would say *the* challenge – confronting modern education.

Perhaps some people may find this too academic: I will be a little more practical. Thirty or forty years ago it was fashionable to say that although we had shed the medieval superstition of Christianity we should retain its ethical standards. The Sermon on the Mount and the Golden Rule would not lose their authority whatever we might come to believe about their author. People had some excuse for talking like that then: there is little excuse for the people who still talk like that, with the grim years of intervening history from which to learn. No really religious man would defend religion on the grounds that it makes people behave properly, but it is quite certain that men will not behave properly without it. The problem of juvenile delinquency (which is modern jargon for what our forefathers called Original Sin) has set some very unexpected people talking about what the Church ought to do for Youth. Educationists have a duty to proclaim standards that are positive and free from ambiguity, not only in the realm of thought and belief, but also in the realm of conduct, which proceeds of course directly from what we think and believe. It is all very well to talk about 'education for freedom': Stevenson's character was being just as free when he was Mr Hyde as when he was Dr Jekyll.

I have time to make one other point: I will make it briefly. We speak very glibly about democracy, but have you noticed how many people nowadays are challenging, apparently quite unconsciously, the beliefs which are fundamental to democracy and without which it cannot exist? Thomas Jefferson said that it was a self-evident truth that all men are born equal. Today it is becoming increasingly fashionable to deny the doctrine of the equality of man, because people have ceased to hold the religious convictions which form the only context in which that doctrine makes sense. Of course men are not equal in ability: it is a waste of breath to prove that. They are equal in value. But when we use the word 'value' we postulate a valuer. What state or what ruler really values all men equally? You will find none in history, not even in the democracy of Athens, except where you find men who believe in a Heavenly Father who has created His children all different, but values them all equally. To put it differently, if you regard men as ends it will be quite obvious to you that they are equal: if you regard them merely as means it will be quite obvious that they are not.

Whether, then, we consider the problem academically, or socially, or politically, the same answer stares us in the face. We must recover our beliefs if we are to establish a sense of purpose and give a concrete meaning to our abstract slogans. That is true of our society and it is, of course, true also of the education which serves it. If we are to be rescued from a half-baked materialism, from a further decline in standards of behaviour and from a cynical abandonment of democracy, we shall be rescued only by an education which has recaptured certainty of purpose and clarity of aim – that is, by a Christian education. And that means, not education in Christianity, but education by Christians.

BEFORE YOU CAN SAY 'JOHN ROBINSON'

(An address to a Conference of Methodist and Quaker Headmasters, Headmistresses and School Chaplains) April 1965

I have manifestly no qualifications which would entitle me to pose as an expert, in this assembly, on such formidable topics as the words which appear in the theme of this Conference – Crisis and Theism and Morals. The experts are coming later. My function, as I see it, is to launch the discussion in the shallow end, so that we may acquire confidence for the profundities that lie ahead. I want, therefore, to state briefly in outline the urgent, contemporary problem of those who try to engage in religious education in 1965 and the years that lie ahead, years in which, I imagine, our problems will grow more acute before the pendulum begins to swing the other way, if that is what is going to happen. When I speak of religious education I am not concerned specially with that part of our education in which, so Sir Richard Acland tells us, We Teach Them Wrong: I refer to the general concept, which I am sure that we all share, of relating all learning to Truth, and carrying out the whole technique of personal relationships which is what we believe education to be, in the light of Christian postulates about God and Man and Life.

I need do no more than *state* certain facts which are sufficiently obvious; there is no time to illustrate them properly. We have to work in a society which is becoming increasingly hostile. In the Press, and on wireless and television, no-one now feels it necessary to defend himself for being an atheist or an agnostic, and this is fair enough. Why should he? But the boot is on the other foot. The assumption is that only a fool or a knave can now be a believer or pretend to be one. The tendency has been well illustrated in a recent notorious and all-too-frequent programme of sub-satire on television. On that programme belief has suffered from jeering and parody and a sort of assumption that it has been examined and rejected on its merits by glib journalists and slick 'personalities'. On the occasion of the doubt of T. S. Eliot, to whom the members of this group of ageing adolescents duly paid their sedulous tributes, I watched with pleasure as they leaned over backwards to avoid referring to the indubitable fact that most of his cherished values were things that they normally delighted in rejecting with as much public contempt as possible. And I thought, in my schoolmasterly way, what a splendid thing it would be if the clevers could be made to write out a thousand times, 'T. S. Eliot was a Church Warden'.

But you will tell me that I am digressing and I don't see how I could deny it. I am speaking of the increasing hostility which surrounds us as Christian apologists. I will take another example, this time from the field of education. In the last few years there has developed an attack (which is growing more vocal almost every day) on the practice of holding daily assemblies for prayer in the State Schools. Professors of Education, no less, have proclaimed the emptiness and hollowness of such a ritual, and demand that in this secular age children should no longer be subjected to it. Of course there have always been people who talked like that. But am I right in thinking that they have grown more confident, and more insistent, and more numerous in the last few years? I am sure that I am. All the signs point the same way. There has been a notorious decline in membership of the religious societies at the Universities, but not in the Humanist societies. Soon after the war the Master of my own college at Cambridge told me that the Chapel was not big enough to contain all the undergraduates who wished to attend the College services. Would any College say that today? Are there signs that *we* have lost our nerve a bit in this respect? How many 'religious' schools have reduced the number of their compulsory services in the last few years in response to this trend? And how many have found that their 'understanding' has been rewarded by an increased resentment of the compulsion that still remains? Where is this trend going to stop? But I know that these are fighting words and I expect to be involved in controversy on this theme. So let me make it clear that I know quite well that concession is not the same thing as surrender, and that voluntary services have positive virtues of their own and a very good case can be made for them.

I have said enough to indicate that there is plenty of evidence of the hostility in the contemporary climate. But our problems – yours and mine – are only just beginning. After all, if we have any understanding of our faith, we have always known ourselves to be a minority and we ought to have prepared ourselves for the enmity of those who do not agree with us. Our forefathers coped with the catacombs and the Coliseum; we oughtn't to be very daunted by a bit of television Frost-bite, or by the waspish onslaughts of the prophets of permissive education. But just at this moment, when we are girding our loins and facing the foe, we find that the trumpet is giving an uncertain sound; there are whispers (and more than whispers) from our own lines that some of our armour is getting a little rusty, and our sword is so obsolete that it doesn't matter whether it sleeps in our hand or not. And back at headquarters, we are told there are those who hold that our whole panoply is suspect. Our only really up-to-date armoury, it appears, is represented by the barrage pouring inexhaustibly from Woolwich Arsenal. The only trouble is that it is not always easy to be quite certain in which direction the artillery is pointing.

I had better illustrate what I mean. For the last two years or more I have been arguing that the secular attack on the religious provisions of the Butler Act gives an added raison d'etre to Schools like ours, independent religious foundations. I don't claim any credit for that not very subtle conclusion which I have drawn from the contemporary educational picture. But I now find that both the Bishop of Woolwich and Miss Monica Furlong (an original and stimulating writer on the Christian side) are arguing that, at this juncture, the Church ought to abandon its schools and its teachers' training colleges for the sake of identifying itself more completely with secular society. I don't want to

discuss the merits of that proposal in this paper (though I won't con-
ceal from you the fact that I don't agree with it). I give this example
only to show that it is a guerilla war that we are fighting and one in
which you are as likely to receive a blow on the base of the skull from a
friend as a punch on the nose from an enemy.

I think that I really ought to come out into the open at this stage and
say what I think about all those *franc-tireurs* of the faith – John
Robinson, Alec Vidler, Wren-Lewis, Chris Driver, Monica Furlong,
and old Uncle Harry Williams and all. I think that they are sincere and
gifted people, and that they are doing a good work that needs doing –
some more so than others. They are making people think; they are
acutely aware of the gap between the Church and the World and they
are driving us to seek for ways of bridging it. Whether they can bridge
the gap themselves I often doubt, in spite of the enormous sales of the
episcopal paper-backs. I cannot believe that anyone who can follow
the tortuous processes of thought and involved prose of one of these
writers (guess!) would have any difficulty with the most obscure
Pauline passages in the Authorized Version. I think, moreover, that
they are in danger of becoming victims of a sort of jaunty jargon, just as
stereotyped as the old pious vocabulary, and without the majesty of its
tradition. I mean by that that the unregenerate worldling is likely to be
less put off by a hearty evangelist who wants to preach the gospel to
him in Church, than by a with-it academic who seeks to engage him in
a meaningful dialogue on Meeting Point. Recent writings by non-
Christians seem to confirm this view – notably as articles by Malcolm
Muggeridge in the *New Statesman* and by Marghanita Laski in *Punch*.

I am having to talk in shorthand, so I cannot say more to convince
you that I really admire many of the efforts of all of these writers and I
sincerely believe that the state of the Church would be parlous if it
were not producing such people. But my quarrel with them (a family
quarrel) is that they are too much in tune, not with the spirit, but with
the methods of the age. They have about them, very often, a touch of
the advertiser, of the tub-thumper who over-states for the sake of
emphasis, and this accounts for what I call a sort of journalese in their
presentation of their views. The slogan seems to be, Comment (of

course) is free; fact, no doubt – if there is any – is sacred; but be sure that you have heresy in the headlines! It was not accidental that the publication of *Honest to God* was heralded, not only by a television interview, but also by an article in *The Observer*, a kind of trailer from which you might deduce that a very sensational volume was about to be released. Similarly *The New Reformation?* received trailer treatment, this time (as was only fair) in *The Sunday Times*, where we could read – in what proved to be an appendix in the book – that God is intellectually superfluous, emotionally dispensable and morally intolerable. So a century and a half after Shelley was sent down from this University for writing a tract called 'The Necessity of Atheism' he was vindicated by a bishop – something which would have astonished the clerics who expelled him. Of course the bishop didn't conclude that it was necessary to be an atheist, but he gave the impression, not only in the title, that he might easily reach that conclusion and – as often happens I fear, with those who deal in sensationalism – his apparent attack on traditional theism proved more readable and more easily intelligible than his subsequent statement on the other side. I found the whole thing a little bewildering – like the embarrassing terms in which the same bishop championed *Lady Chatterley's Lover* in the Court case a few years ago about that disagreeable volume.

My contention is that so much of this 'neo-writing' is affected by a subconscious resolve to shock the orthodox and placate the worldling that the effect is out of drawing and will be seen to be so in a few years' time. In the meanwhile we have to continue with our job of religious education, without being rattled, neither burying our heads in the sands of tradition nor rushing down the Gadarene slopes of a with-it-at-all-costs conformity. (If you think that that is a hopelessly mixed metaphor, perhaps I might defend it by explaining that I am advancing the surely moderate thesis that we should emulate neither the ostrich nor the swine.)

I know that it may seem to some of you that I in my turn am overstating my case in the indictment which I have drawn up of the perversity of the contemporary prophets; I ought, perhaps, to illustrate my theme a little. Here are two quotations.

(*a*) 'So conditioned for us is the word "God" by association with a Being out There (with all, in other words, that the anti-theist finds superfluous, dispensable or intolerable) that we have been warned. You must forget everything that you have learned about God, perhaps even that word itself. Indeed, the line between those who believe in God, and those who do not, bears little relation to their profession of the existence or non-existence of such a Being. It is a question rather of their openness to the holy, the sacred, in the unfathomable depths of even the most secular relationship.'

(*b*) 'As God is Immanent and yet Transcendent, so we cannot see the whole Truth, but only an aspect of the Truth, until we have reconciled ourselves to the last final antinomy, that God is both existent and non-existent. We, who are conscious of the supreme Being as existent, and those who are conscious of Him as non-existent, are each of us looking at only one half of the truth . . . and we can surely hope that when we have studied each other's point of view . . . we shall all of us recognize the Divine Governor of the Universe as one who exists, yet does not exist, causes sin yet hates it, hates it yet does not punish it, and promises us in Heaven a happiness which we shall not have any consciousness to enjoy.'

The first of these extracts, of course, is from *Honest to God*. When I read that work I thought that the style of it reminded me of something else that I had previously read, with its daring excursion into heresy and its balancing recoil into a kind of orthodoxy. And then I remembered the work of which it reminded me – that from which I culled my second quotation. It is from a volume of Satire published by Ronald Knox in 1928; the essay from which I have quoted was called 'Re-union all round, being a plea for the inclusion within the Church of England of all Mahommedans, Jews, Buddhists, Brahmins and Atheists.'

I noticed, as I read the passages to you, that you received them both with the same puzzled respect; it is a sobering thing when the accents of parody in one generation become the accents of prophecy in the next.

I find also, in the writings of our theological avant garde, two

147

disquieting tendencies. One is a highly selective citing of Scripture –
a failing, I hasten to admit, to which we are all prone. Old-fashioned
Evangelicals used to talk sometimes as if the only approach that Jesus
ever made to people was the one that he made to Nicodemus; our neo-
prophets tend to choose the story of the woman taken in adultery.
Most people now will agree that you cannot base a general theory of
conversion on the single text, 'Ye must be born again.' I think that it is
equally unsound to base a general theory of morality on the single text
'Neither do I condemn thee.'

The other disquieting tendency is a failure to tell the whole story
when citing the authority of Scripture – for example, the suggestion
that our Lord's last word from the Cross was, 'Why hast Thou
forsaken me?' rather than, 'Father, into Thy hands I commend my
spirit', or the assumption, in the story to which I have already referred,
that Jesus parted from the woman taken in adultery with the words,
'Neither do I condemn thee.' It is really rather important, and relevant
as a basis for morality, that he went on to say, 'Go and sin no more.'
Those of you who try, as I do, to play golf will know what happens if
you don't follow through; the ball in flight deviates from the orthodox.
I detect in much modern writing about the faith the lack of a dialectical
follow-through which leads to a kind of theological slice.

I should like to examine in some detail, though briefly, the appendix
in *The New Reformation?* which is challengingly entitled, 'Can a contemporary person not be an atheist?' In answer to this loaded question
the Bishop sets out the atheist's objections to the concept of God under
these three headings: (*a*) God is intellectually superfluous. (*b*) God is
emotionally dispensable. (*c*) God is morally intolerable. All of these
propositions he concedes, or appears to concede, you have to watch
very carefully – as you would watch a stranger doing card-tricks for
money in a railway carriage – to see the episcopal legerdemain which
substitutes an obsolete picture of God for that normally held by contemporary Christians. When the Bishop answers his own arguments
the card-trick is done in reverse and so the happy ending is achieved,
for those who can follow it all. As I read I found that under each heading the obvious answer to the atheist's claim sprang unbidden to the

mind; the author's answer, later in the chapter, was relatively woolly, involved and unconvincing. For example, God, we are told, is intellectually superfluous because man has come of age and discovered that Laplace was right after all: 'God? I have no need of that hypothesis.' As Bonhoeffer said, 'Man has learnt to cope with all questions of importance without recourse to God as a working hypothesis.' That is absolute enough. When did it happen? It used to be a platitude to say that man's mental ability had outstripped his moral development, and like most platitudes it was true. Of course, if you limit your 'questions of importance' to the field of the natural sciences and mathematics you need have no recourse to God as a working hypothesis, though men like Eddington and Jeans seem to have found it a helpful concept that a world which can be apprehended only mentally found its origin in an Eternal Mind. But the intellect asks other questions, concerned with purpose and value: Do the stars run blindly? Is there a will of God? Is there a far-off, divine event to which the whole creation moves? Is the Good anything other than the Expedient? It is no good calling such questions meaningless, or irrelevant. The fact that people ask them is part of the evidence and makes them relevant. Young people will ask them of you and me, if we do our jobs, and what are we to say? That God is intellectually irrelevant? To tell you the truth, it is this talk about Man Come of Age that really worries me. It is only a metaphor and it is already overworked; overworked metaphors become dangerous. This one suggests that all that was wrong with the tower of Babel was that men did not know how to build it high enough, but now we can do it. And so man, proud man, looks into the vacated heavens and sings, not the Te Deum, but 'Anything you can do I can do better.' Suppose Man Come of Age is really a dangerous, clever adolescent? We, of all people, know after all that one of the most dangerous conditions in juvenile delinquency is produced by the adolescent's premature belief that he has grown up. (What, if anything, ought our age to make of the injunction that we ought to become as little children?)

Of course Dr Robinson, who is a Christian man, doesn't leave it there. He brings God back again in another guise. 'The one who is superfluous as a hypothesis,' he says, 'becomes all too personal as a sub-ject of encounter.' But a humanist might be forgiven for arguing that no-one would ever say that unless he had been brought up among Christian assumptions. Huxley, for example, who described theism as 'The last fading smile on the face of the cosmic Cheshire Cat' is likely to look with some scepticism on the prospects of any such 'encounter' with vestigial feline traces, so we are no nearer to 'meaningful dialogue' with him.

It was the same with the other two headings. 'God is emotionally dispensable; we must grow out of immature ideas about Providence.' As I read this argument I instinctively quoted Paul: 'What shall separate us . . .' When the Bishop had finished erecting his parody of mature Christian belief he gave us the solution triumphantly in these words of Tillich, 'No situation whatsoever can frustrate the fulfilment of his ultimate destiny, that nothing can separate him from the love of God which is in Jesus Christ.' How can a Christian believe that God is emotionally dispensable? Of course we grow out of childish ideas, like expecting that prayer will get us through an examination for which we have neglected to work, or enable us to make a century in a House-match, or – to take the Bishop's example – save us from an air-crash even though the pilot is inefficient. But these are times in life when our faith is vain unless it can cast our burden on the Lord. What have we to say in the face of death? Most of us in Boarding Schools have known times, I expect, when a member of the School lay very close to death and the whole community was involved in the attendant emotion. At such times, if God is emotionally dispensable, He is not real at all. Under this heading, too, we shall need more convincing answers to give to the questions of the young if, as I think, we are to be true to our faith. Do we find God 'emotionally dispensable' when we have to tell a boy that his father has died?

The statement that God is morally intolerable is simply a perverse way of saying that an inadequate philosophy of suffering is inadequate. The Bishop's conclusion is well expressed: 'What it means to believe in Love as the final reality is to be discovered, not in the absolute con-troller who allows the suffering, but in the crucified, transfiguring figure who bears it.' Yes, but this is surely the classic answer of Christian men, given over and over again by recent apologists like C. S. Lewis and Dorothy Sayers. Why all the atheism?

The question that confronts us, as working Schoolmasters and Schoolmistresses concerned with Christian education, is this. What can we give to the questions of the young that will not appear to them to be woolly and evasive? We know, of course, that we mustn't be authoritarian, or anything like that, but may we be positive? In the great concert of life, is there any score, or must we all play, all the time, by ear?

It would be pretentious and impertinent of me to try to tell you what are the details of the irreducible creed of the contemporary Christian. May I, as I finish, state three principles as my personal belief about the way in which we ought to approach our eternal task in a changing climate of thought? First, at the heart of our thinking we must have what is, after all, the irreducible creed of any Christian, contemporary or not: 'Jesus is Lord.' Everything stems from that. And I make bold to say that careful study of the relevant documents has led me to the conclusion that Jesus was a theist, that he believed God to be intellectually relevant, emotionally indispensable and morally tolerable, to say the least. He said to his own age: 'Ye believe in God; believe also in me:' and he says to our age, 'You believe in me; believe also in God.'

Secondly, I believe that we are in great danger, in education, from the philosophy of permissiveness, at a time when the psychologists have grown out of it. The young need positive (not bigoted) guidance in behaviour and they need it in belief too. That consideration should guide us in determining how much, or how little, we ought to put before them by way of creed. And thirdly, we of all people need at this time to avoid the role of the weathercock, blown about by every wind of doctrine. We have seen, in this century, the needle of the theological compass swing from Schweitzer to Barth and back again to Bonhoeffer (if 'back' is the right word). It is not irrelevant, I think, to point out that you don't become permanently contemporary simply by abandoning a traditional metaphor. We were told two years ago that it wasn't honest to God to think of Him vertically. I was delighted to read a sentence the other day of that very fashionable thinker, Teilhard de Chardin, in which he spoke of his experience of God as 'The majestic, down-flooding Reality.' Down-flooding? So some of our hymns become respectable again.

We have to be aware of contemporary thought, of course, and sensitive to it, and willing to learn from it, but we must try to see Truth, not only *sub-specie aeternitatis* but also on the scale of Christian history; we should not be content to wait for the next compelling paper-back translation from the next prophetic German to restore the balance, but we should seek to maintain the balance by reading, not only the exponents of 'worldly holiness', but also Bunyan's *Pilgrim's Progress* with its City of Destruction and Vanity Fair. For the first word of our gospel was not 'Conform' but 'Repent', and the first word of our traditional worship is not an affirmation of our adulthood but a confession of our sins and of our need of God's forgiveness. We have to seek, humbly and in faith, to be instruments of the Spirit, who is neither rebel nor reactionary, but the same, yesterday, today and for ever.

HYMNS IN SCHOOL WORSHIP

Address given to the 1965 Conference of The Hymn Society

In the nature of things, a schoolmaster spends most of his time addressing people who know less about what he is talking about than he does. He has chosen his career with this principle in mind. By the time that his audience's knowledge is in any danger of approaching his own not necessarily very exalted level, he arranges that they shall be taught by someone else. When unavoidably, he finds amongst his pupils the occasional precocious specimen whose level of knowledge is a potential source of embarrassment, he has a number of devices, born of discipline out of experience, for silencing or circumventing them. This accounts for the air of complacency and even of omniscience which people find so unendearing a characteristic of my profession. So you will understand that, when I sat down to try to prepare this paper, the question which loomed largest in my mind was how on earth I had managed to put myself – and you – in this predicament. For you are all experts on the subject of hymns and my credentials are those of the merest amateur, as I shall shortly show.

My first instinct, of course, was to crib wholesale from the brilliant outline of the history of hymnology with which Dr Erik Routley has adorned the new hymn book, *Hymns for Church and School*. And then, with a sinking feeling, I realized that the distinguished author is not only the holder of high office in your Society but might easily be presiding over this gathering this morning. And I felt as some modest enthusiast about our railway system might feel if, having promised to give a talk to a Railway Society, he discovered that the name of the chairman was Bradshaw, and that a vote of thanks would be proposed afterwards by Dr Beeching. (When I found that Dr Routley wouldn't be here after all, it was too late.)

In the presence of experts, subterfuge is futile. I can only put my cards on the table – it is a pretty thin hand – and ask for your indulgence. My one really high trump is that I am a Methodist, a son of the Manse, indeed, who from his earliest days attended two services every Sunday as a matter of course (and, I may say, without complaint), and whose native air from infancy was the magnificent legacy of song which is the Methodists' true liturgy. So I cannot help having some knowledge of hymns, though my love of them is mixed with nostalgia, and associations which have nothing to do with theology or poetic merit, and my criticism is, for that reason, almost entirely unreliable. As for school worship, I have a certain experience of that – about thirty years of it in two Methodist boarding-schools; and that experience, I suppose, if I can interpret it intelligently, must be of some relevance to the theme of this paper. But I am conscious that it is a limited experience, and I am cautious of erecting any general conclusions on it.

It is true, as you know and as I therefore must admit, that I have made several attempts to write hymns. All that I have proved by these attempts is that it is extraordinarily difficult to solve the problem – which someone has got to solve – of writing hymns in this age. There seems to be something about contemporary methods of expression in verse which is incompatible with the regular shape and rhymes which traditionally (though not invariably) a hymn demands.

The only successful – that is to say, widely read – poet who appears to me to have the equipment for writing hymns is Mr John Betjeman, and I wish that he would do it. I can only assume that he is the angel who fears to tread where fools like myself, however tentatively, rush in. As a matter of fact, the only successful hymn that I have written, in my opinion, was composed for a service which I drew up in an effort to meet liturgically the challenge of the thought-forms employed by the Bishop of Woolwich in *Honest to God*. The first hymn in that service is designed to cater for the Bishop's statement that we must stop thinking about God vertically, and look for him, not up, but down. This is its first verse:

> O worship the Thing
>   Mysterious below;
>   In what terms to sing
>   We don't really know;
> The image of Father
>   Has now been destroyed,
> So we will preach rather
>   The Gospel of Freud

I give you that example in all honesty so that you may recognize in me an incurable frivolity which prevents me from appearing among you in the pretentious guise of a 20th-century inheritor of the mantle of Charles Wesley.

There is one advantage that I have in talking about this subject, and that is that I work in a school where the congregational singing is exceptionally good. I make this claim without hesitation because I cannot possibly be held to qualify for any credit in the matter. It is a simple fact of experience that visiting preachers, especially those who come from other schools, hardly ever fail to comment on the quality of the school's singing.

I believe there are two reasons for their singing well. First: about 50 per cent are Methodists, and possibly half of these come from good Methodist homes, so they have been brought up in a tradition of good, hearty singing. Secondly, the shape and acoustical properties of the Chapel are such as to make congregational singing easy.

I am most anxious not to be misunderstood at this point. I am not claiming any merit for our boys other than that they sing well as a congregation. I don't mean to say that our services are any better, or our worship any more effective, than those in any other school. I certainly don't mean that the congregation is any more virtuous. There is no necessary correlation between fervour in singing and depth of religious feeling. I never feel that 'Abide with me' at Wembley is a very significant indication of the religious condition of the nation, and anyone who has listened to the Welsh crowd at Cardiff Arms Park before a Rugby Match should know the difference between soulful singing and spiritual quality. I remember a friend of mine, a Methodist minister and a keen follower of Rugby Football, who found himself at Twickenham once in a pocket of Welsh invaders. He was moved and thrilled by the rendering of devotional hymns before the match, and he picked out one tenor in particular as being a man of considerably saintly character. He was sadly disillusioned when the game began, and his sensitive ears were assailed by a stream of language, emanating from the same tenor voice, consisting of what Chesterton once called 'theological expressions which hold no doctrinal significance'. 'Angel voices ever singing' is the first line of one of the hymns that our boys sing best. It is very far from a description of the singers.

But I would make the point that they sing well because they enjoy it, and they enjoy it because they do it well; quality and enjoyment are interdependent and both are needed if the singing of hymns is going to contribute to worship. Indeed, I would go further. I believe that when a number of boys, met together in the context of the school chapel, feel themselves at one with each other and lose themselves in communal singing, even apart from their consciousness (or lack of it) of the meaning of the words they sing, they partake – though not necessarily at a deep level – of that mystery which we call the numinous; this may be one of the tasks, however simple, that set the soul who does them free. I think of one member of our sixth form who calls himself an agnostic and who ostentatiously refrains from any devotional act when he comes into chapel, but who sings every word of every hymn with manifest enjoyment. I firmly believe that in doing so he is being more really religious than he knows, or would care to admit, or than anyone ought to tell him!

I think that I ought now to face the question of compulsory school services – for it is in the setting of such services that I am considering the singing of hymns. I will tell you why I think that they are not just defensible, but positively right. I don't mean, of course, that there is no room for voluntary services, which have their own very precious atmosphere; but we are a religious foundation, and on Sundays we have two services which the whole school attends, and I am not disposed to be at all defensive about it – though I don't think that there is any magic about the number *two*.

In the first place I should argue that a school is a place in which most important things are compulsory – unless, indeed, it is one of these temples of permissiveness where the Ego is supreme and nobody is made to do anything. We are more traditional than that. We compel people to attend classes, to play games, to be present at all meals, and to be in bed (we hope, asleep) for an appropriate period every night. This compulsion, on the whole, is taken for granted and not resented. In such a community there is an obvious correlation, implicitly, between importance and compulsion. I mean, the boys feel that you expect them to do the things that you consider important, and you leave them free to please themselves in affairs that don't matter so much. If you make them do French and Rugby Football and insist that they turn up to lunch, and then tell them that they needn't go to chapel unless they want to, they conclude, not that religion is too sacred and personal to be made compulsory, but that you believe that French, football and food matter very much, but that religion matters less. If you make them do them all, as a matter of course, they accept the whole thing as, at worst, part of the inscrutable adult pattern of values.

Of course, there is no such thing as compulsory worship; but then we don't go in for forcible feeding. What there is is a compulsory opportunity for worship, like the opportunity for eating. We accept the undoubted fact that the school in chapel will operate, as it were, at different levels.

Some will experience real devotion; others will enjoy only a good sing. But we are thankful for what we get. We recognize that it is our duty to make the whole thing as painless as possible, to keep the services short and try to make them interesting; and I honestly think that the congregation has very little to complain of. Sunday is a day which is full of freedom for them. The only demand that we make is that they meet together twice in the day, for about 40 minutes on each occasion, and experience, as a community and as individuals, some contact with the mystery which surrounds all life. Pascal said, 'There are two types of men who can be called reasonable: those who serve God with all their hearts because they know Him, and those who seek for God with all their hearts because they don't know Him.' That is what we should like to be a description of our school congregation; why should we encourage those who have prematurely abandoned the quest? Secondly, the voluntary principle creates all sorts of avoidable tensions. In a close community like a boarding school, few activities are as voluntary as they may seem to be. A boy is subject to all sorts of social pressures; he may refrain from going to chapel because he belongs to a tough gang and lacks the courage to be nonconformist; he may attend in a self-conscious, pious pose, because he is proud of being a nonconformist. In this realm the community may save the young from unnecessary friction and harmful tension by taking the decision for them, and I think we ought to do it. I speak, of course, for schools that are religious foundations, so that people know what they are in for when they attend them, I think, provided that they can be conducted by people who are convinced and sincere and who will (if you see what I mean) not try to make them too religious.

I must get back to hymns. I want to say a little about the principle of 'having a good sing', by which I mean the notorious tendency of congregations to sing tunes, not words, and indeed to have a very vague idea, if any, of the statements to which they are committing themselves, often fortissimo.

This is something to which the modern generation is very accustomed. In the world of popular music the words often hardly bear examination. The best of them spring from a folklore which is quite remote from contemporary life. The obvious example is the mythology of negro spirituals. A few years ago the Black and White Minstrels made very popular a song which repeated this line 'Michael, row the boat ashore – Hallelujah!' I once asked a sixth form who Michael was, and what he was doing in a boat. None of them knew and none of them thought it mattered. I asked whether it would do equally well if they sang, 'Michael, show the goat the door: it's peculiar.' They thought that it would. Thousands of people in a football stadium every Saturday throughout the season express vocally their desire to be of that number when the saints go marching in. I believe that in Liverpool there is a superstition to the effect that the Fourth Gospel was written by a centre-forward.

One of the inept things that Adam Faith said in his television discussion with the Archbishop of York was that the church was at fault in its hymns, because the lyrics were incomprehensible. My point is that a great many popular songs are rooted in a mythology which people no longer understand, but that this doesn't stop them singing them.

Since this is part of the current pattern, one ought not to be surprised that it is practised also in chapel. Boys love the Welsh tune Cwm Rhondda and they love to sing the last verge at the top of their voices – the one that says 'When I tread the verge of Jordan, bid my anxious fears subside'. When you tell them that it is about death, they don't doubt it, but they don't see the relevance because they are accustomed to singing tunes and not words.

Sometimes, we have an evening service without a sermon, which consists largely of expounding hymns and then singing them (the sort of thing we did last night, only shorter). I like to explain to the school, about every three years, George Herbert's magnificent poem, 'Teach me, my God and King', so that they may understand the striking imagery of a verse that none of them understands at first sight:

A man that looks on glass
  On it may stay his eye,
Or if he pleases, through it pass
  And then the heaven espy.

They are glad, I think, to know what it means, although it is extraordinary how quickly they forget.

I believe, in spite of all that I have said about this habit of singing meaningless words in the pop-world, that we ought to pay more attention to the words of the hymns that we ask the young to sing, and to make sure that they are dignified, good theology, and appropriate to the congregation. There is some appalling phraseology in some hymns which slips by unnoticed because of the tune with which it is linked.

I will limit myself to a few examples.

We have in the Methodist book a splendid hymn about the Emmaus road:

> *Lord Jesus, in the days of old*
> *Two walked with thee in waning light:*

The third verse begins, regrettably –

> *Perchance we have not always wist*
> *Who has been with us by the way.*

'Perchance' and 'wist' – no one ought to be asked to sing such archaisms, which were already archaic and self-conscious when the hymn was written.

Among my aversions are hymns which employ a kind of sentimental Victorian version of Arthurian chivalry as their mythology (some written, I ought to say, by public-school headmasters in the last century) and hymns which call on the young to rescue the Eternal Truth from the collapse into which it will fall if they don't rescue it:

> *Rise up, O men of God,*
> *The Church for you doth wait:*
> *Her strength unequal to her task,*
> *Rise up and make her great.*

You recognize the pampered youth taking his hands out of his pockets and having half a mind, in a renewal of transient idealism, to devote a little of his spare time to the task. I can't hope to command much agreement with my next example, but I cannot share the enthusiasm with which many sentimental, middle-aged people listen to boys in a public school chapel singing Bunyan's 'pilgrim-hymn' –

He who would valiant be,
Take a good look at me . . .

or words to that effect. I believe that the Christian way is to be entered on more humbly than that; I much prefer Bunyan when he is writing prose.

There are some hymns that are inappropriate for boys for different reasons; hymns which call for dedication in terms which are either irrelevant, or make too great a demand on the sincerity of a whole congregation. I feel like this when I hear a crowd of young North Country materialists singing

Take my silver and my gold:
Not a mite would I withhold.

There are sentiments which are too deeply devotional to be sung lightly or sung often. I don't know how many other hymn books besides the Methodist include that beautiful Indian hymn which begins

One who is all unfit to count
As scholar in thy school.

If you know it, you will know that it contains sentiments of self-abasement, expressions of the humility of holiness, which few congregations ought to be called – or allowed – to sing except in very special circumstances.

I have already said that I don't believe that we ought, in school, to sing 'When I survey the wondrous cross' very often, but I do think that there are occasions when it can be sung without impropriety. I remember one of them vividly. It was a Sunday evening service which we had, of an experimental nature, as near to Easter as we came in term time last year. After an orthodox opening to the service the choir sang, as an anthem, the moving Spiritual 'Were you there when they crucified my Lord?' Then, instead of a sermon, two boys and a master spoke for five minutes each, the first giving, in a loose kind of verse, the point of view of Pontius Pilate, the second speaking as Judas, and the third (from the pulpit) as Simon Peter, in the events which led up to the Crucifixion. Before each speaker, one or two relevant verses from the Gospel were read. The atmosphere which had been created by this quite unexpected approach was memorably emphasized when the whole congregation then sang 'When I survey'. I can remember no more impressive example of the contribution of a hymn to school worship.

Another example which comes to my mind is the singing of 'God be with you till we meet again', which has become the traditional way of ending the last service of the school year. I know that it may be mixed up with nostalgia and sentimentality and all sorts of things at which it is easy to laugh, but there may be true religion in these things and I believe that there is, for many of us a valid spiritual experience as we unite in that corporate expression of our membership of one another, in the context of the school Chapel.

I have said that I believe that good theology ought to be one of the elements of a hymn. Anyone brought up on the hymns of Charles Wesley would have to say that. I cannot resist reading to you what I believe to be one of the most perfect examples of the hymn-writer's art. It is Wesley's superb hymn on the Church Militant and Triumphant. In some hymnals it begins 'Let saints on earth in concert sing', but I shall read it to you in the version in our Methodist hymn-book (824):

Come, let us join our friends above
That have obtained the prize,
And on the eagle wings of love
To joys celestial rise:
Let all the saints terrestrial sing,
With those to glory gone;
For all the servants of our King,
In earth and heaven, are one.

One family we dwell in Him,
One Church, above, beneath,
Though now divided by the stream,

The narrow stream of death:
One army of the living God,
   To his command we bow;
Part of His host have crossed the flood,
   And part are crossing now.

Ten thousand to their endless home
   This solemn moment fly;
And we are to the margin come,
   And we expect to die;
Ev'n now by faith we join our hands
   With those that went before,
And greet the blood-besprinkled bands
   On the eternal shore.

Our spirits too shall quickly join,
   Like theirs with glory crowned,
And shout to see our Captain's sign,
   To hear His trumpet sound.
O that we now might grasp our Guide!
   O that the word were given!
Come, Lord of hosts, the waves divide,
   And land us all in heaven.

I know of no better hymn than that. I agree with Bernard Manning that even the deservedly popular 'For all the saints', on the same theme, must take second place to Wesley's poem.

But lo, there breaks a yet more glorious day;
The saints triumphant rise in bright array;
The King of glory passes on his way ...

There is something thrilling in that verse, but it is the thrill of Tennyson's 'Morte D'Arthur'. Wesley is all Biblical.

I have strayed a little from my theme, I know, because this is not a hymn for schools to sing very often (if at all). But I wanted to make my point about a great orthodox doctrine of Christianity being greatly expressed in religious verse. Having said that, I want to say something quite different.

I know a fine Christian preacher who is so wedded to orthodoxy that he will hardly choose a hymn unless it is either by Charles Wesley, or translated from the German by John Wesley. I once said in public in his presence, that I thought highly of the hymns of Whittier; I thought that he was going to have to be helped out of the room. But I do indeed think highly of those hymns, 'Immortal Love', 'O Lord and Master of us all', 'Who fathoms the eternal thought?', 'Dear Lord and Father of mankind'. Think of that fine verse –

In joy of inward peace, and sense
Of sorrow over sin,
He is his own best evidence
His witness is within.

Everyone – of any theological school – could sing that, from Wesley to Woolwich.

It is important to remember, I think, that we ought not to look for the whole Gospel in every hymn, and many not very pretentious offerings have their use. I have heard a chapel full of boys singing with great enjoyment and some fervour 'All things bright and beautiful' after someone had said to them, in announcing it, 'This is really a hymn appropriate for young children – and none the worse for that.' In theory nothing could be more offensive to boys of 17 than to ask them to sing that sort of thing, but it didn't work out like that. It is strangely moving, in the opening moments of a carol service, to hear sophisticated (not to say hardboiled) adolescents singing without any apparent embarrassment

For he is our childhood's pattern,
Day by day like us he grew;
He was little, weak and helpless,
Tears and smiles like us he knew.

164

In the mysterious realms of schools and of religious expression there are hardly any rules that do not know any exceptions. This is true at least of singing hymns, but preachers ignore at their peril the self-conscious sophistication of the young. The most terrible words that I have ever heard in a school chapel were uttered by a well-meaning visiting preacher who had forgotten his own youth. He had chosen some sickly illustration, of herosim, in a house-match, which was bad enough. He proceeded to pile Pelion on Ossa by describing his hero in these spine-chilling terms: 'He was only a little boy,' he said: 'He was only seventeen.' The waves of resentment from his indignant congregation could be felt.

Before I conclude I want to say something about the future of hymns. We have got somehow to solve the problem of writing new hymns. The preoccupation with setting familiar words to popular tunes is, I believe, wrongly conceived. Who really wants to sing 'Love divine' to the Z-car tune, or 'Abide with me' to two electric guitars and a vacuum-cleaner? In our school chapels, at any rate, most boys have a sense of what is fitting, and they know the difference between the Judgment of God and Juke Box Jury.

If they fall for the blandishments of pop-experiments, it is not for long. Anyhow, they like the familiar hymn tunes and they love singing them – sometimes too much. I don't mean that we ought not to have good contemporary hymn tunes: but if we could also fittingly set new words to the tunes which they already respect, we might help them to understand what they are all about. We need neither iconoclasm nor die-hard-ism, but a judicious blend of the contemporary and the traditional, for we have to do with something which is the same, yesterday, today and for ever.

I have already mentioned one grave obstacle in the way of writing new hymns – that the contemporary idiom in serious verse is un-friendly to the regular metre and rhymes which we generally find needful in hymns. I find another and even greater obstacle in the fashionable current idiom of theology. It is one thing to sing about the panoply of God; it is another and a very different thing to make a joyful noise about the armoury of Woolwich Arsenal. If God, as we have just been told, is intellectually superfluous, how can we sing

> *Thou art the Truth, Thy word alone*
> *True wisdom can impart?*

If He is emotionally dispensable, it is no good crying to Him for those in peril on the sea; if He is morally intolerable, we shall find no comfort in the Rock of Ages, cleft for us, and when the darkness deepens, He will not be there to abide with us in the shadows. Would you join with much enthusiasm in a hymn which began

> *Eternal God of everything*
> *To whom we tentatively sing,*
> *O image that has got to go*
> *Since Dr Bultmann tells us so . . .?*

Hymn singing cannot really be indulged in unless faith is stronger than doubt; if the old simplicities are believed to have lost their validity: if in an age which is more scientific than poetic we no longer understand, as our fathers understood, that mystery can be conveyed only in metaphor; then hymn-singing is bound to flag. It is clearly unthinkable that we should allow the modern age to believe that the only appropriate language in which we can praise God and pray to Him is that of the 18th century – even though that was when they did it best; but when the new Watts and Wesley appear – as they must and will if we are to be faithful to the contemporary guidance of the Spirit – they will write in some other terms than the woolly and worldly scepticism which does duty today as the accent of faith. All this is very reactionary, I know, and it is probably true that I am trying to put too much weight on the unfashionable end of the see-saw. I certainly have very slender qualifications for a technical theological contest, but I believe with all my heart that there is a balance to be redressed.

I said at the start that I was conscious of the difficulty of the task that you set me; I am even more conscious of it at the end. I have stretched my terms of reference beyond breaking point, and I have trespassed in fields in which I have not been invited to walk and where I have no right to be found.

Let me try to make amends by at least finishing on a relevant note. I believe that hymns make a very important contribution to that mysterious thing, school worship. Not all the things we invite boys to sing can be appropriate to all their needs, or represent the experience of more than a fraction of the congregation. Of course much of the joyful noise that they make owes more to a sort of corporate youthful euphoria than to any more specifically religious emotion. But all education is experiment and exploration, and so is this aspect of it. What I have called corporate youthful euphoria *is* a kind of praising of God, who has made us to be dependent on one another and who likes his children to be happy and to say so. Sentimentality and nostalgia may be – even though shallow and fleeting – an apprehension of what I referred to earlier as that mystery which we call the numinous; they may lead boys to associate with the chapel some alternative to that self-centred materialism which is the besetting evil of our affluent society. This, at any rate, is something which I believe that I have experienced, not seldom, in school chapels.

IN A SCHOOL CHAPEL (1947)

A few days ago I sat in a School Chapel and experienced the unique variety of emotion which is peculiar to such places. I was attending a special service in memory of the Old Boys who gave their lives during the war. I believe that it is worth trying to record the thoughts and feelings of those forty minutes, not because I imagine that there was anything strikingly original about them: on the contrary I have no doubt that they were shared by most of the congregation – but because of my conviction that we need in these days above all things to try to find some coherence for the emotions about which we are least coherent.

Inevitably my starting-point was the recollection of the personalities of my friends amongst the fallen. I shall say nothing here of the sense of personal loss which has left no circle of our society untouched; I shall say little on the hackneyed theme of the Lost Generation, of the rich promise squandered in war leaving barren the hard-won peace. Only a poet or a prophet can tread these paths without sententiousness or vain repetition. From these painful reflections my mind moved to the soul-searching question, 'Why did they die?' and – more bitter still – 'What has been achieved by their dying?'

I reminded myself first of all that the boys whom I knew were candid and free from humbug. They entered on their ordeal without any of the splendid illusion of 1914. They did not thank God for matching them with the hour; they did not count it rich to die in a shattered tank or a burnt-out aircraft and they called for no bugles to blow out over their sacrifice. They went into battle open-eyed and they knew that it was hell: in our thought about them we must be equally honest. We have no right to shame them with any shallow sentimentality.

Why did they die? Not for the Atlantic Charter, not to make a land fit for heroes to live in. They knew the cheap trickery of such phrases; they did not imagine that six years of carnage could prove the inevitable prelude to the New Jerusalem. They had no room for heroics, certainly, and they did not think much of heroism. They fought ungrudgingly, but in a sense unwillingly. They could do no other and no words could pay adequate tribute to what they did – and they did not like doing it.

These heirs of disillusion fought, and died, to give us a chance. It was not that the war would make things better, but that without war there would be no more opportunity of making things better. The cause was not progress, but the survival of civilization: the enemy was not alien rule but chaos and devilry and the negation of every human value. I have said that above all they were honest and that we must be honest about them. They did not, most of them, fight and die to save Christianity, which in any case needs no saving and cannot be defended by force: but consciously or unconsciously they were champions of Christendom and they saved Christian values from the catacombs. They would not, of course, have used this pretentious language; they would have used, if pressed to put their feelings into words, the common coin of the British tradition and spoken of decency, tolerance and the enjoyment of the simple things of life, but that is what their words would have meant.

They achieved their objective, it seems. The forces of chaos were beaten from the field and, though the price was high, the victory was achieved: civilization survived – or at any rate gained the condition of its survival. But the price, I was reminded, was not something inanimate and replaceable: the names on the list which I held in my hand stood for boys whom I had known and who now are not here. Something precious has gone from our midst and we cannot talk glibly about 'the price' as though we had paid in a coinage which we could recover with the economy of a few years.

King David was a very old-fashioned man, living in the unenlightened days of the Old Testament, but he knew the value of human sacrifice: he saw the sacredness of the water which was brought to him at the risk of the lives of those who loved him. I wondered in that Chapel, and I wonder now, what would be the impact on our society of the realization that the days in which we live are sacred because they have been purchased for us with blood. Our debt is to the dead, but we can pay it only to the living. Our creditors will not press us for payment; the dead have no votes. But they stand in silent judgment on the post-war world and we are in a very solemn sense compassed about with a great crowd of witnesses.

How do we stand before that jury? I thought of the pitiful tale of the past months. The dismal catalogue of failure and frustration rose to mock the sacrifice of the dead. I saw the comradeship of the Allies in war give place to the shabby manoeuvrings of the Great Powers; I saw the unity of purpose in our own land crumble before class struggle and party strategy; I saw the crisis of the nation exploited to make debating points for Government and Opposition. And as a background to it all there rose the voices of the scientists, those former prophets of a confident humanism, warning us of the perils of the atom in the light of which we see at once our mental triumph and our spiritual meagreness. And I knew that in the court of the dead we stood convicted of moral bankruptcy.

I am tired of hearing and reading academic discussion about British survival, as though it were an interesting problem of economics. I am tired of a Press which uses the bitterness of our present predicament as a stick with which to beat either the present Government for the inefficiency of its rule or the last Government for its legacy of muddle. And I believe that thousands of my fellow-countrymen are equally tired of these things. Henry James's words were never truer than they are today: 'we need a moral equivalent for war'.

The war is still on: the victory which won for us our chance was a vital achievement but the end of the struggle is not yet. In the not very remote past the people of these islands have shown the world that in times of crisis they know how to close the ranks. The threatened chaos of the last decade was not a greater menace than this: we weathered that storm by abandoning party differences and responding to a clear National lead. In 1940 the issue was clear and the victory was primarily and fundamentally a moral victory long before it could become a material victory. I do not believe that I am alone in asking whether the time has not come for the same solution. The question is again a moral one and a moral triumph is the first condition of economic success. Failure does not mean fundamentally the vindication of capitalism and the discrediting of socialism: it means the betrayal of our past and of our future, the dishonouring of our unspoken pledges to our dead. If there is any vision and leadership left in British politics then let us hear again the call to unity: I do not believe that it will go unheeded. But if we have so used up our spiritual resources that we can observe our present squalid recriminations without shame then we had better prepare ourselves for the fate which awaits those who have apathy and sloth in the soul. And let us spare the fallen the mockery of our empty mourning.

NEO-MATINS

*(Found in the crypt of a College Chapel in Cambridge: significant for
the liturgy of the emerging Church.)*

PRIEST

When scientific man turns from tradition and the superstition
which his fathers have transmitted to him and comes to church, he
knows neither why he comes nor what he will find there, but in the
language of depth psychology (he is taught) he may preserve his
intellectual self-respect, and in affirming his nescience he does that
which is lawful and right.

Fellow gropers, and worshippers of the modern idiom, the scriptures
say many intolerable things to us, in obsolete terms, about sins and
wickedness which we ought to confess; but I urge you to turn your
back upon such outmoded exhortations and to join with me in an
affirmation which is acceptable to contemporary thought-forms.

*[Here shall be said this affirmation, the congregation standing erect to
symbolize Man Come of Age.]*

We proclaim together that we have grown out of grovelling and
penitence. We bear no resemblance at all to lost sheep. We have
followed consistently the devices and desires of our own hearts and we
know of nothing for which we ought to apologize. We have done those
things which seemed good to our enlightened scientific intellects and
we have left undone those things which, in our wisdom, we chose not
to do. And in this manner, in the light of modern knowledge, we
propose to conduct ourselves in the days that are to come. We are men.

[*And everyone shall repeat 'Are men' to emphasize the dignity of adult humanity.*]

[*Then shall be sung hymn No. 1.*] [*Tune: 'O Worship the King.'*]

O worship the Thing
  Mysterious below;
In what terms to sing
  We don't really know.
The image of Father
  Has now been destroyed,
So we will preach rather
  The gospel of Freud.

The Church with too much
  Addiction to prayers,
Is quite out of touch
  With modern affairs.
While tied to a myth it
  Is ancient and square
The Church must be with it –
  The Bishop is there.

Thou give to each priest
  A scholarly prod;
One cleric at least
  Is honest to God.
Our creeds may be foolish
  But hope is in sight
The Bishop of Woolwich
  Is putting it right.

What science may teach
  As currently true
The Churches will preach
  Obediently too.

Hypotheses splendid
   They'll gladly adore,
Till fashions are ended
   And fads are no more.
         Amen.

[*Then shall be read, as the first lesson, the following Psalm.*]

The Lord (to adopt for the moment a word of doubtful significance) is not a shepherd, nor any such image proper to a pastoral society. I do not want to think of him (to employ a calculated anthropomorphism) in any such terms. An authentic religious experience, whatever that may be, has nothing to do with green pastures or still waters. Nor is it appropriate to speak of restoring the soul, now that we have arrived at a psychosomatic concept of the nature of man. The paths of righteousness convey no picture of an environment into which we need to be led, since worldly holiness is something which we experience wherever we may be; it goes without saying that there is no comfort to be derived from such bucolic emblems as a rod and a staff. Surely German theology, meaningful though unintelligible, shall pursue me all the days of my life, and I shall dwell for ever in the satisfaction which comes from a condition of enlightened bewilderment.

[*Here endeth the first lesson. Then shall be sung Hymn No. 2.*] [*Tune:* '*Eternal Father . . .*']

Eternal ground of everything
   To whom we tentatively sing;
O Image that has got to go,
   (For Dr Bultmann tells us so)
Set heirs of modern science free
   From metaphor and simile.

Not supernatural, afar,
   But latent in all things that are,
When we, enlightened in our doubt,
   Can get on very well without,

We are delighted to be free
From metaphor and simile.

So, at Thy non-existent feet,
    Thy liberated people meet,
And in Thy temple make it clear
    They do not know why they are here,
Proclaiming proudly they are free
    From metaphor and simile.
                    Amen.

[*Then shall be read the Second Lesson.*]

A certain man had two sons. The younger said to his father, 'Father, give to me the share of your possessions which is earmarked as my inheritance.' And he took the money and went into a far country. And there he gave himself up to worldly holiness with practitioners of something which was known as the New Morality. But after a time he became a victim of the capitalist system and had difficulty in obtaining gainful employment. It is at this point that the story takes a tragic turn. For the youth rejected the privilege of having become Man-Come-of-Age and failed to understand that, being utterly fatherless, he was for that very reason nearer to his father than ever. He weakly returned home and actually apologized for his show of independence. The father, being a product of a pre-scientific, ignorant age, met him halfway and was delighted to have him back; indeed he gave way to senile sentimentality and hyperbole, describing the young man as having been dead (in his state of worldly holiness) but as now being made alive again (in his condition of abject dependence). The elder brother showed an equally deplorable failure to understand the situation and actually blamed the younger for ever having left home at all. The whole story is a classic example of the sort of religious error which was commonly found in pre-Bonhoeffer documents.

[*Here endeth the Second Lesson. Then shall follow the Non-Creed and certain anti-collects of an acceptable nature. After this shall be sung Hymn No. 3.*] [*Tune: 'Lord, Thy word abideth'.*]

No especial grace is
  In religious places;
Natural behaviour
  Does not need a saviour.

There's no richer treasure
  Than we find in pleasure;
Pluck and eat the apple!
  Keep away from Chapel!

O what liberation
  In this proclamation,
Licensing enjoyment
  Priestly unemployment.

When the bells are ringing
  And the choirs are singing,
People who are grown-up
  Go and pick the phone up.

Oh what a prodigious
  Bore are the religious!
Proudest people fear them,
  Never venture near them.
                    Amen.

[*Then shall be preached a sermon, if possible in German, explaining
under three headings that the New Theology is* not (*a*) *Humanism,
(*b*) Pantheism, (*c*) Atheism. And the best of Teutonic luck to the
preacher. After which Hymn No. 4 shall be sung.*]

O God, our help in ages past
  (Or so the Psalmist said),
We now can face the stormy blast
  Without external aid.

We read upon Tradition's page
  Of things that God has done;
But now that man has come of age,
  He meets his fate alone.

In ignorance they used to grope
  To find the perfect plan,
But nothing is beyond the scope
  Of scientific Man.

And if to pieces he should blow
  The world he has not made,
At least he can be proud to know
  He did it without aid.

The ages past extolled the Name,
  But not the years to be.
Hear Thine enlightened child proclaim
  He has no need of thee.

Of paradox behold the sum
  (Perhaps you'll think it odd)
When godless we have quite become
  We shall be near to God.
                              Amen.

[*Then shall the Priest dismiss the people with the following admonition.*]
  Go forth into the world to proclaim that the only obstacles to the
Truth are Religion and the Church, and may the Depth of all Being
grant you a modern outlook and a muddled mind, and keep you from
coming here again to meet with retarded and probably hypocritical
people. *Amen.*

AUTHORITY AND VALUES

(*Address to the Headmasters' Conference*) *October 1964*

I would ask you to believe that it is with considerable diffidence that I talk about this subject to this audience. It is a common practice for people in our job to speak with great confidence on a wide variety of subjects, and most audiences have been conditioned by their school-days to listen to headmasters with a respect to which the quality of our thinking may or may not entitle us. But here I have to speak on an educational topic to a gathering of professionals and I have no special claim to do so. The experience of most of you is at least as great as my own, and your practice, for all I know, may be far more successful, so I shall address you because I have been told to and not because I think that I have any claim to. So much by way of apology for standing here, but I make no apology for my views, some of which, I have been told, are not quite contemporary. Only I must stress that I am having to scratch the surface of a pretty profound question.

I think that we are in danger, in this age, of being a little neurotic when we talk about the problems of authority. Authority has *always* been a problem for any adults with a sense of responsibility for the young. Some kind of tension between the generations must exist. The adolescent has to grow up in a society which has values about which he has not been consulted; in a number of ways he is required to toe a line which he has not drawn. He has always felt that the short cut to personal identity lies through revolt. The adult knows that he has to provide a background of security for the young and that the two extreme enemies of that security are remoteness and possessiveness; on the one hand, the cold shoulder, and on the other hand, what may be called the hug of death. In a healthy atmosphere between the generations he treads delicately, like Agag, between these extremes.

This inevitable conflict between the generations is sharpened today by the teenage cult, a product of contemporary media of advertising and of influences which have discovered in adolescents a profitable market. It is to their interest to flatter the young, to put an inflated value on their tastes and standards, to encourage their revolt against authority and to herald the dawning of the permissive age. So, for example, the less reputable part of the Press will describe a girl of 13, sent home from a modern school for wearing too much make-up, in terms which would be excessive if applied to Joan of Arc. A few months ago I saw a boy interviewed on BBC Television. His headmaster had compelled him to have his hair cut by an imported military barber, and the afflicted child had absented himself from school for the rest of the day because, so his bereaved mother said, he felt that his appearance was now too ridiculous for public display. We can only marvel at the Spartan fortitude with which he acceded to the request of the BBC that he should reveal his condition that evening, presumably to millions of viewers. I have a cynical friend who said not 'fortitude' but 'bribery', as if someone had been raising the wind for the shorn lamb. I fear the sad truth is that no one is too young to find a television camera irresistible. I am having to talk in shorthand, but these two illustrations surely show that responsible forces are exercising an irresponsible influence in the matter of authority, in implicitly inviting the public always to sympathize with the rebel in an imperfectly understood disciplinary conflict.

As a result of this – and many other factors – authority seems now to be on the defensive and I suppose that many of us are disposed to look at this question defensively in this session of our Conference. For the popular view of us is inaccurate. To most people, I think, the 'image' of this Conference (in the contemporary jargon) is of a fairly stiff-necked lot of reactionaries, a sort of block of the Old Chips, educational Bourbons who have learned nothing and forgotten nothing, yearning to exercise a Victorian authoritarianism in the modern age. But really most of us are no more disposed to be domineering than any other cross-section of our generation and as tempted by the charms of permissiveness as any other well-meaning adults. And so there has grown up an attitude to authority, within the profession, which can be summed up fairly and without parody in the following proposition: 'It is not our job to tell the young what to do, but to give them their heads and leave them free from direction and stand by to pick up the pieces.' I have read of this recently as the considered view of two professors of education, and you cannot get higher than that – can you? What I want to say is that I believe that to be heresy – you might call it the Gadarene heresy, which regards the educational process as allowing your charges to run violently down a steep place and providing first-aid at the bottom. I suppose it is old-fashioned of me to think of my job in pastoral terms and to prefer to regard myself as a shepherd rather than a swineherd – even a Gadarene swineherd. The trouble today is not that there are too few shepherds: there are too many, of a kind. It is not that the hungry sheep look up and are not fed, which is bad enough. They look sideways, or down, and they *are* fed – by the irresponsible hirelings who gladly fill the gap in authority when those who ought to be shepherds have abdicated.

The difficulty about permissiveness is that when the young run violently down steep places they drag others with them. Samson would make a good representative type for adolescents. He was very strong and very impetuous and his hair was never quite the right length. And he involved other people in his self-destruction and no one could pick up the pieces. Those who entrust children to our care have a right to expect that we shall not leave them to be the victims of one another's experiments in ethics. After all we teach by precept as well as existentially. 'The burnt child dreads the fire' is a very useful cliché but it would make a very poor school motto. Please God we shall keep some of them out of the fire altogether, even if we have to exercise a little authority to do so – or do we stand by and pick up the ashes?

I have called permissiveness a heresy. Let us remember what a heresy is. It is not a falsehood, but a part of the truth exclusively emphasized at the expense of the whole. Heresies arise when one important truth has been neglected and needs restating and the Pharisees in all ages are the orthodox who refuse to learn from the heretic. So let us acknowledge our debt to the Gadarenes, as I shall try to do in turning now, very briefly, to the positive side of my thesis.

I have three positive things to say about authority, and I can state them quite shortly. I must do no more than state them. First, the young have a right to authority and we must not deny it to them. However independent and even rebellious they may seem, part of their security is an inarticulate philosophy of crisis, when an adult will step in and deal with the emergency, *before* it has reached Gadarene proportions. To put it in another way, they have a right to expect to be able to dial 999 and to reverse the charges. Secondly (and this is what we learn from the heretics) they have a right to the *right kind* of authority and to be free from the wrong kind. The most profound thing ever said about authority was this: 'You could have no authority over me unless it were given.' That is what the developing personality which we call the adolescent knows in his bones. He is accepting authority all the time in mountaineering or in music, in mathematics or athletics – from someone whose commands he respects because he knows them to be rooted in a discipline and an expertise which carry their own conviction. We have all seen this kind of thing happen. The authority that he rejects is a kind of arbitrary imposition of mere personal preference: 'When I was your age we didn't do that kind of thing' or 'Why? Because I say so.' And if we have any proper educational standards we shall be proud to see him reject such pretentious authoritarianism. (I recognize that, in some circumstances, it might be right for the right person to say, in the right way 'Because I say so.')

The third thing is to be able to point to the source of authority. It is easy enough when the technique is a limited one like climbing a mountain or playing the violin: what when it is a matter of ethics and values and the techniques of living? It is here, I think, that those of us who serve in schools which are Christian foundations have an immeasurable advantage. For Christ is not only the source of our authority about life; he is also our example in the exercise of authority. In the Christian framework we may know absolute points of reference (so that our authority is neither arbitrary nor merely personal) and in the Christian spirit we may find charity and a due regard for persons, in a discipline that can never become merely mechanical. And so the yoke may be easy and the burden light. I do not myself think that the problem can be solved (except temporarily and by exceptional men) in a humanistic context. The abdication from authority, where it exists, is not essentially (as it has been called) a failure of nerve, but a failure in faith. 'Example,' said Burke, 'is the school of mankind.'

THE TRUTH ABOUT CRICKET

OR

THE SEVEN AGES

(*Speech to the Lancashire County Cricket Club Dinner*)

It is, of course, a tremendous privilege for me to be invited to return to the County for which I have a birth qualification to talk about cricket. Indeed I have been waiting all my life for Lancashire to take note of that qualification and now – rather late in the day – it has done so. At least, I assume that that is why I am here tonight. I can't think of any other qualification that I possess.

I must admit, at the outset, to feeling more than a little bogus at appearing before this distinguished and knowledgeable audience as an expert on cricket, especially when I reflect on my predecessors. I remember some years ago speaking at the annual dinner of a County Cricket Club. As I recall I appeared as a rather late substitute for Herbert Sutcliffe, who had had to cry off. It was a new experience. It so happens that I had never previously been asked to take his place in a cricket context. I reached the depths of embarrassment when the distinguished peer who was President of the Club turned to me during Dinner and said: 'You must forgive me: I am very ignorant about cricket. Whom did *you* play for?' All sorts of answers presented themselves to my mind. I nearly said 'Lancashire'. I once made a hundred for Lancashire before lunch. I was not only playing for Lancashire: I *was* Lancashire. I made 185 before I was out for the tenth time. And then my brother went in. He was Surrey. But I rejected that answer; it wouldn't, I thought, be strictly honest. And I rejected all the other lies that offered themselves to my fertile imagination. The Chairman had said he was ignorant, but he hadn't said *how* ignorant. I said, evasively, 'Wait till I make my speech. Then you'll know.'

I was reminded of an incident in the experience of Stephen Leacock, the Canadian humorist. He was a professional academic, a Professor of Economics, and he held the degree of Doctor of Philosophy. He relates that he was once crossing the Atlantic in a luxury liner. The most conspicuous and popular passenger was a famous and very beautiful film actress. One day on the voyage the Purser came to him and said 'You are *Dr* Leacock, aren't you?' and he said that he was. 'Would you be good enough to help us?' said the Purser. 'Our film actress has injured her leg and she would like a doctor to examine it.' Dr Leacock had a short, sharp struggle with his conscience; then he accompanied the Purser to the actress's cabin. But he was too late, he said; he had already been preceded by two Doctors of Divinity.

Ladies and Gentlemen, I am only too conscious that I also am the wrong sort of doctor, and I am as embarrassed as Dr Leacock no doubt would have been if he had been compelled actually to exercise a professional expertise which he did not possess. After all, it is quite simple for someone like Mr Brian Close to capture your attention whenever he sees it wandering. A little judicious name-dropping will do: 'On the third day of the Lords Match I turned to Ted and said . . .:' or a firsthand account of Fred Truman's uninhibited comments when the umpire was unable to see things from his point of view – nobody can fail if he can resort to such expedients. But what do you care about my recollections of the unprecedented profanities of some nonentity in the slips on Parker's Piece in 1938?

When in doubt, I always turn to Shakespeare (who had a birth qualification for Warwickshire). And though, for reasons beyond his control, he said nothing about cricket, he gave us a clue to what he *would* have said about cricket, in the celebrated passage in *As You Like It* which is known as 'The Seven Ages of Man'. For of all games and pastimes cricket is the one which endures throughout a man's whole life. As William Wordsworth (of Westmorland) said, 'The child is father of the man,' and there is no reason to suppose that he was not thinking when he said it of man's unending enthusiasm for cricket.

So I propose to arrange my thoughts about the great game around the pattern of the seven ages of cricket.

First, the infant. There isn't a great deal to say under this heading, since one of the many drawbacks of infancy is that this stage of our lives is almost totally devoid of the beneficial influences of the greatest of all games. Of course, for the favoured few, the offspring of the game's aristocracy, the shadow of Lords may be said to lie across their privileged cradles. As the poet[1] has said,

> *The high and mighty of the earth*
> *If they've been registered at birth,*
> *Before they die expect to be*
> *Elected to the MCC*

But this choice destiny awaits only the élite. Others face a cricketless infancy, except in those rare cases where an exceptionally fanatical father, and an exceptionally pliable mother, put the favoured infant in a carry-cot and conduct him every Saturday afternoon to a corner of the pavilion where the smell of bat oil in his nostrils and the excuses of dismissed batsmen in his ears, may become the earliest and most formative influences of his life. There is one relevant story that occurs to me, though it has an unhappy ending. It tells of a wealthy and devout cricketer of fifty years ago who had his own cricket ground on his estate. As soon as he learnt that his first-born was a son, he did two things. He had him christened Wilfred Rhodes, and he planted laurels at one end of the ground where they would prove most advantageous to someone bowling left-arm round the wicket. The fact that the boy grew up to be no sort of bowler, and right-handed at that, is one of those ironic twists of Fate to which only a Sophocles or a Russian novelist could do proper justice.

> *Then the schoolboy*
> *With sandwiches in pack and scruffy book*
> *Lying in wait to cadge an autograph.*

---

[1] From the *Batsman's Bride*.

If there is little material in the first stage, there is so much in the second that it will be difficult to keep it within bounds. For it is now that cricket becomes a passion, and a way of life; a vision and a dream. It is not too much to say that it becomes a religion. I was reading recently the reminiscences of a man who says that when he was a boy he used to pray every night for the Surrey team, in batting order. Sometimes he would get so carried away that he found himself saying, not only 'God bless Strudwick, God bless Hitch,' but also 'God bless Leg Byes; God bless Wides'. And, talking of religion, one of the most genuinely devout comments I ever heard of is attributed to Walter Brearley, the Lancashire fast bowler. He had heard that a player called A. E. Knight, a very religious man who played for Essex, was in the habit of praying before he went in to bat. Brearley was furious. I'll report him to the M C C,' he said. 'It's bloody unfair.' His language may have been unorthodox, but no-one could have demonstrated more vividly a passionate belief in the efficacy of prayer.

There are many aspects of the devotion to cricket, which we feel in the second stage, that are akin to the higher life of man, associated with religion and aesthetics, and everything that appertains to the soul. There is the submerging of self as we identify ourselves passionately with a cause, with the bloodless battles of country and county. There is the beautiful quality of admiration, an appropriate hero-worship not yet poisoned by the cynicism and premature worldliness of adolescence. When I was a child Hobbs and Sutcliffe were to me what the Olympians were to the ancient Greeks: if I had been told that in the course of my life I should meet both and get to know one of them well I should scarcely have believed it to be possible. My special hero was Ernest Tyldesley, because he played for Lancashire. (I lived in Cambridge, and I hadn't seen Lancashire since I left this[1] town at the age of two. The very name of the county contained everything that was mysterious and romantic.) I shall never forget my indignation at what the selectors did to Tyldesley. In one golden summer he made more centuries in succession than anyone had ever done before, so that the selectors, in spite of their anti-north bias, were compelled at last to include him

---

[1] Southport.

in the England team. He made 81 and they promptly dropped him –
never again did I altogether believe in justice.

This stage is also the primitive period of embryonic cricket, and
superstition about the game. No-one is a true cricketer who has not
played at that jungle level, where a number of boys who have never
been introduced played together in a park; where the wicket-keeper
crouched alertly with a coat with which to trap the ball and whoever
happened to have the ball at the end of one over bowled the next one –
and where the odd belief stoutly persisted that if you hit the ball with
the back of the bat, you were out. A similar level, though more
organized, exists in schools, where people with little talent for the game
play an odd variety of it, under compulsion, for some mysterious
reason. There the hazards of batting are added to by the fact the umpire
is the next man in and is wearing a pad to prove it; in such circumstances
an appeal from the bowler is the merest formality. I remember an over
in one such game which was delivered with so little control that it
contained – counting all the wides and no-balls – seventeen deliveries,
three dismissals and a retired hurt. (I reflect rather complacently that
probably the Yorkshire Captain, when he addressed you, was unable
to recount anything similar in his personal experience of the game.)

The third stage is that of the young player and now we move into an
altogether more self-conscious and sophisticated period. Cricket is now
an affair of ties and blazers and fancy caps. The young cricketer has
grown out of his artless desire to identify himself with Freddie Truman
or Ted Dexter or Colin Cowdrey; instead he enters on the Narcissus
stage and labours to build up his own image. He studies technique
and concerns himself with such matters as footwork and the raising of
the left elbow. (And truly if either elbow is to be lifted this is the
better one and this the more harmless study. All too soon he will become ambidexterous.) Now, too, he goes to school with the journalists
and the commentators and learns the mysterious jargon of club cricketers. There is no need for me to illustrate this; anyone who has listened
to Mr Peter West talking about Barber's 'leggers' will know what I
mean.

It is at this stage that some of the less endearing habits of mature cricketers begin to be admired and emulated. There used to be a curious idea about that cricket was good for the character; people invented sickly metaphors and talked about playing with a straight bat on the wicket of life, as if a straight bat had something virtuous about it and hooking and cutting were somehow shameful. 'It isn't cricket.' Now I am, as you will have gathered, particularly mad about cricket, but let it be *loved* for the right reasons and let it be *saved* from cant and hypocrisy. No game is particularly good for the character, or bad for the character either. Games are simply vehicles for revealing the character that you already possess. We have all met cricketers who were sportsmen, and cricketers who were not: there are those who will go when they are out and others who will wait and hope to profit from some deficiency of the umpire. There are those who accept defeat gracefully and those who are as prolific with their excuses as any golfer!

There are many pleasant stories associated with this stage – the brash adolescence of the cricketer; I have time for only two of them. The first tells of Dr Grace asking a complacent young man who was playing for his side what number he usually batted. 'Anywhere you like, sir,' said the youth, smugly. 'I've never made a duck yet.' 'Better go in No. 11,' said the Old Man. 'You've not been playing long enough.' The other story is of a University player who was bowled neck and crop by a Yorkshire professional in the first over of the game, for all his gorgeous cap and the immaculate public school manner in which he played forward. 'That was a good ball,' he said, patronizingly, as he passed on his way to the pavilion. 'Ay,' said the bowler, drily, 'it was wasted on thee.' I know that you have all heard that story before; the only advantage that a speaker has over his audience is that he can tell any story that appeals to him and claim that it illustrates his theme.

By the end of this stage it will be decided, probably for all time, whether the young man is a cricketer or not. For there are many siren songs to lure him away from the game – more than ever before. There is the mobility conferred by the internal combustion engine to tempt him in a restless generation which loves to change its position in space and confuses movement with progress. There are social pursuits and the unaccountable reluctance of young women to sit and watch a cricket match patiently; there is that self-centred pursuit of the un-attainable that men call golf. But if he can rise above all those lures, if in spite of all temptations to inferior recreations, he remains a cricketer, in success and in failure, if he enjoys fielding and takes only a second-ary interest in his own average – then he has the root of the matter in him and we can follow him to the fourth stage.

The fourth stage covers the best period of a cricketer's life, through maturity to the veteran class. He is still a slave of the game, but like any experienced servant he has learnt to manipulate things so that his service affords him the maximum of comfort and enjoyment. For example, he has studied the psychology of captains and he applies it to preserve himself from the embarrassments and even humiliations which may be the lot of the less experienced. I had better illustrate what I mean.

No self-respecting cricketer likes to go in last. It is not so much that he may be left high and dry without a partner; there are compensations about being not out; indeed, if the bowler is some hostile and erratic West Indian, for example, there are compensations in running out of partners without taking strike. What hurts the sensitive soul is the Captain's tacit assumption that such an event will cause no measurable loss to the side. Your mature player has a formula which prevents him from ever finding himself in such a position. For, suspecting the Captain's intention to send him in last – and experience has developed in him an instinct in such matters – he remembers casually that he is not in very good form at the moment and would just like to go in much later than usual. 'As late as No. 8 if you don't think that too absurd,' he says, laughing lightly. No decent man will be brutal enough, after that, to put him any lower than No. 7 in the order. There is bound to be some youth in the side who will give loyally when he finds himself yet again at No. 11. Similarly, the mature cricketer, if he is fortunate enough to be given the ball doesn't lightly surrender it; he has a device which will guarantee him at least two more overs after the Captain has deter-mined to take him off. Listen to this carefully; you may find it very useful. The technique is this. He goes into the field wearing two sweaters, a heavy one, which he removes when he goes on to bowl, and a light, sleeveless one, which he retains. When the critical moment comes, at the end of an unsuccessful over, when the captain approaches with the intention of dispensing with his labours, he anticipates the usual formula of insincere gratitude, by asking for an alteration in the field for his next over. Then he removes his second sweater, hands it to the umpire, and walks off purposefully to his place in the field. Do you think that any normally civilized captain will have the courage to subject him to the humiliating exercise of putting on his sweater, until he has bowled at least two more overs, however expensive? Of course not. And when the supplementary spell is over the captain will be so demoralized that the bowler will be able to retain the initiative by asking to be taken off (conveying the slightest hint that the captain has over-bowled him) and indicating, not too reproachfully, that he would really rather *operate* from the other end 'if he should be needed again'.

But, of course, the cricketer who has reached the fourth stage realizes before long that the only really satisfactory thing is that he should himself be the captain, and he will achieve this happy consummation even if he has to run a team of his own to effect it. Believe me: I know. Now he really has the game satisfactorily under his control in every department. He will place himself in the batting order with a due regard to the nature of the enemy bowling and its probable freshness, or lack of it, at various stages of the innings. As for bowling, he intends to occupy one end most of the time himself and he will have selected his team with a view to having enough people to supply variety at the other end but not so many as to be forced to interfere with his own rhythm. In the matter of fielding, too, he will not have to leave anything to chance; he will not, for example, have to appear himself in an exposed position. When a Dexter or a Bland is batting someone else will have to field at mid-off. (I once had an interesting letter from a Mother about cricket. It read, 'Please see that John stands at mid-off as the hits don't come very hard there.' I thought that, as a combination of ignorance and self-centredness, took a good deal of beating.) I remember one experienced captain who used to field invariably at first-slip. He used to stand very straight, and as the bowler ran up he could edge imperceptibly to his left. Safe in the lee of the wicket-keeper he would watch benevolently while anything smacked beyond that player's reach sped harmlessly down to third man. He went through a whole season without dropping a single catch. Indeed he actually dismissed two batsmen when, in each case the only partially successful intervention of the wicket-keeper had so reduced the pace of the ball as to render the catch virtually unmissable.

Of course captaincy brings its own problems. He is now the man who must persuade someone to go in last and he must face the disagreeable necessity, when the worst comes to the worst, of offending a sensitive team-mate. Here he has only his acquired experience and cunning to guide him. The one principle is that he must not at any cost, choose to antagonize the owner of an indispensable car. And he must know how to anticipate such ploys as those which I have already described. For example, he must know the counter to the two-sweater gambit, in enforcing the reluctant resignation of an experienced bowler.

He will have some puzzles to solve which have never come the way of Brian Close or Mike Smith, in their very limited experience of captaincy. For example, he may have a young fast bowler who fancies himself as a budding Wesley Hall, and who asks for seven fieldsmen behind the bat, all in catching positions. This field is well known to cricketers as the Carmody field and you may wonder why I have suggested that it would present any problem to Messrs Close and Smith. But they have never had to provide this aggressive umbrella from a team which includes four non-bowlers and two cases of advanced myopia. It is in such contexts that cricket is a real test of character, as the captain steels himself to place, in the cannon's mouth, seven incredulous protesting and vulnerable comrades.

But the time comes in the life of every cricketer, however keen, when he can no longer perform with dignity, or even safety. It may be a matter of physique. Nature, in its remorseless advance, may endow him with circumferential proportions which cause the ball to disappear from sight before he can really determine, with accuracy, whether to play forward or back. As one such veteran said, sadly and succinctly, 'When I can see them I can't reach them; and when I can reach them I can't see them.' Or it may be that failing eye-sight renders his exertions in the field quite unrealistic. There is a pathetic anecdote about a player of this kind who had not held a catch for two seasons and people were beginning to notice it. He was standing statuesquely at third man, peering interestedly towards the centre of operations, when a fast long-hop was directed by an eccentric batsman high in his direction, possibly off the back of the bat. By an odd coincidence his evasive shufflings took him into the path of the ball. By what can only be explained as a miracle he perceived the sphere at the eleventh hour and, clutching at it for support, he effected the catch. His pleasure at this almost forgotten experience was unbounded. He tossed the ball proudly from hand to hand and then sat down, still clutching his prize, to await the arrival of the next batsman. But what arrived was first slip, who panted angrily, 'Throw it in, you silly old fool. It was a no-ball and they've run three already.'

After such experiences there is only one thing left for the devoted cricketer. He moves into the fifth stage and becomes an umpire. In this capacity, as he has been saying for years, no deficiency of sight or hearing is recognized as being a serious handicap.

The umpire is an indispensable dignitary of quite immense authority. By tradition his decision is never questioned – or hardly ever, though I am thinking now of one exception, in wartime cricket when anything was possible. A friend of mine, a keen cricketer who enjoyed the advantage of commissioned rank, was batting for his company against a rival unit. He played forward to a bowler who was delivering prodigious in-swingers and received the ball satisfactorily on his front pad. In response to a half-hearted appeal he glared menacingly down the wicket and was relieved to see that the official ignored the bowler's not very hopeful question. Preparing to receive the next ball, he was surprised to hear an apologetic cough from the slips, followed by the still more apologetic comment, 'Excuse me, sir, you're out.' He pointed majestically down the wicket. 'What do you mean?' he said. 'He hasn't said anything.' 'You're looking at the wrong umpire, sir.' Swinging round to square leg, the indignant subaltern saw the umpire with his finger pointing steadily to the sky, like a water-diviner in reverse. The batsman thought of all that he had been taught in a good school about unquestioning obedience to the umpire, and rejected it. He searched for a formula and found it. 'Put your bloody finger down,' he said, 'it's nothing to do with you.' Outranked, the umpire came smartly to attention and the game continued.

While I am speaking of umpires I want, in all seriousness, to make an appeal on their behalf. At the higher levels, at any rate, it makes great demands on their knowledge, their judgment, their concentration and their stamina. There are occasions also when it makes great demands on their character and my appeal is that they should be given more support than they are at present being given. In the matter of judging the fairness or otherwise of a bowler's action the present situation is intolerable. How can it make sense for a fast bowler to be at the same time top of the bowling averages and excluded from the English team because his action is suspect? Why should one umpire, conscientiously carrying out his appointed task, have to incur the odium of pronouncing so important a verdict on a professional cricketer? I saw a television programme in September in which Dexter proved quite conclusively, to me, by means of photographs, that Griffiths throws the ball. In the sensitive atmosphere of international cricket why must it be left to a single umpire to carry out the delicate business of criticizing a leading member of a visiting team and causing his virtual removal from the match in the middle of a vital Test? There are enough disadvantages about living in a scientific age. Why can't we enjoy the available advantages? Everyone in first-class cricket knows which are the bowlers with suspect actions. They should be subjected to a series of tests at Lords. Photographs of their action at every stage should be studied and a committee of experts should pronounce an authoritative verdict. All that would be left to the umpire would be to call the occasional throw. Any bowler who was considered to be turning into a thrower would simply be reported and sent to headquarters for testing. In quite a short time, I believe, a situation would develop in which no serious cricketer would hazard his future by throwing. And umpires would be rescued from a very distasteful responsibility.

I should like, also, to see journalists adopting a far more constructive and responsible attitude to the game's officials. We live in a permissive age and there is no shorter cut to cheap and easy popularity than to espouse the cause of the rebel and attack authority. Having undermined the position of authority you then blame it for not doing its job. Umpires suffer a good deal from this nasty tendency. I object strongly to television and radio commentators who take it on themselves to question the umpire's decisions. And I object very strongly to the ignorant verdicts of the sensation-mongers who masquerade as sporting journalists in many of our newspapers. There was a very glaring example of what I mean in Australia last month. Various journalists presumed to attack an Australian umpire who ruled that Jones must stop bowling because he was following through too straight and cutting up the wicket to the advantage of the bowlers from the other end. Now it is perfectly plain that the official was at great pains to do the right thing and to do it in the right way. He warned the bowler and he warned the English captain before he made his ruling. But this failed to appease his critics, who were looking for an incident so that they should not be reduced to reporting the cricket. Anyone who knows anything about the game knows that a bowler bowling fast, left-arm over the wicket can easily trespass on forbidden territory in his follow-through. Anyone who knows the composition of the English attack, with its reliance on off-spin, can assess the urgency of the problem in this particular context. The umpire would have been very much to blame if he had taken no action; having taken it, he is entitled to the absolute support of all who care about cricket and not just about journalism.

I want to say something else which applies at all levels of the game, and I say it knowing it to be very controversial. In my opinion the umpire is entitled to the help of the players in a difficult decision. If he gives a man out caught low down in the slips, and the fieldsman knows that he took it half-volley, it is only right for the fieldsman to explain the position, and most people accept this view. I maintain that a similar obligation rests on the batsman. If he gets a faint touch, with glove or bat, and the ball goes through to be caught by the wicket-keeper, he ought to help the umpire in his decision by setting off for the pavilion without question. He knows that he was fairly out and that should be an end of it. The fact that he was dismissed unjustly last week is neither here nor there. Every match is a new situation; this bowler and this opposing team have a right to justice. The umpire is there to see that they get it and every self-respecting man should be interested in helping him in his task.

The sixth age of the cricketer, the post-umpire stage, is that of the legislator. He is a very high-powered figure, indeed; an ex-player of great eminence, or a peer of the realm, or a Field-Marshal. Many thoughtless cricketers deplore the activities of such people. 'There's nothing wrong with the game,' they say. 'Let them leave it alone. If players only played as we did in our young days there'd be no need to muck about with the laws.' Such enthusiasts take no account of the history and evolution of the game. If no-one had ever mucked about with the laws, what a different spectacle our national pastime would present. The bat would still be shaped like a hockey-stick, since that was the most appropriate kind of weapon with which to cope with bowling which was fast, underhand and along the ground. If you don't believe that underhand bowling could ever be fast, let me remind you that there is a legend of one such delivery which evaded the efforts of two fieldsmen, then passed clean through a coat with which a spectator tried to stop it and killed a dog on the other side. (This tale proves, if it proves anything, that people have been telling lies about cricket for a very long time.) The wicket, at that time, consisted of two stumps only, with a bail across the top. The third stump was added because the ball kept on passing between the two stumps without dislodging the bail, to the intolerable distress of the bowlers. The outstanding bowler of the period, and presumably therefore the chief sufferer, was a professional with the formidable name of Lumpey. I have often pondered on the probably uninhibited terms, mainly Anglo-Saxon in derivation, with which so robustly named a bowler would express himself in the circumstances which I have indicated. Whatever those terms may have been, they effectually secured the introduction of the third stump.

With such stirring examples in mind, let us think kindly of the legislators and wish them well in their task. May they have the vision which is open to change, and may they have the wisdom to change slowly and reluctantly and even belatedly. For cricket is a sphere in which every man, without controversy, ought to be a conservative, with the classic motto that if it is not necessary to change, it is necessary not to change. Above all, let legislators turn a deaf ear to all requests that they should bring cricket into line with the spirit of the age. It is one of its virtues that it is a slow game, an anachronism in these graceless, hurried days; the time will come, if we will have faith and patience, when the age will come again into line with the spirit of cricket.

The seventh age, said Shakespeare, is second childhood, mere oblivion. In cricket it consists of garrulity in the pavilion, of endless repetitition of improbable anecdote, of great lies about a golden age that never was and of an inability to stop talking about cricket. Before you are confirmed in your suspicion that I have reached it, I will sit down.

Verse – Grave and Gay

ON TO OECUMENICITY

Onward Christian Soldiers,
　　Full of dash and pep,
Marching to the battle
　　Bravely out of step.
When the trumpet calls us
　　Forth against the foe,
In the same direction
　　(Roughly) we will go.

Never mind the allies
　　Falling at your side;
Other sects may perish,
　　Lord, with us abide!
Anglicans and Baptists
　　Never will be missed.
God (we will not doubt it)
　　Is a Methodist.

Onward Christian Soldiers
　　To the holy war.
Never mind the crisis
　　Business as before!
Men and causes perish,
　　Churches fade and wane:
To our small tradition
　　Loyal we remain.

For a world in darkness
Never can appal
Us in our small corner,
Looking at the wall,
Of our common mission
Sadly unaware.
Brightly gleams our banner
Pointing here and there.

THE CHURCH DIVIDED

The parish Church upon the right
   Stands stiffly, too aloof to know
The little Chapel opposite,
   And past them both the people go,
Not caring that on either hand
   The Church's two foundations stand.

The chosen people at their prayers
   Sit huddled in their ones and twos:
The preacher in his pulpit stares
   Upon a wilderness of pews.
But why should Chapel people care?
   The Church (thank God) is just as bare.

Though Jesus came on earth to die
   And our redemption dearly bought,
The 'decent godless' folk go by
   And do not give a second thought.
The people are not seen to meet
   At Church in Coronation Street.

How long, O Lord, how long our shame,
   Who hide the undivided light,
Guarding our small, especial flame
   While people perish in the night?
Save from the lesser loyalty
   And make Thy children one in Thee.

WHAT IS MAN?

And what is man? That creature he
   Of Physics and of Chemistry,
The mighty Molecule; his brain packed full
   Of formulae. O man, proud man!
A little crack on your developed skull
   And deep-browed Einstein is a Caliban.

And what is man? The climax he
   Of ages of Biology.
Up to man, Nature traced her patient graph;
   And when the last line of his tale shall fade
Who will be left to read his epitaph?
   'This man was the animal that made the grade.'

And what is man? Epitome
   Of measureless futility;
Playing with pomp his unimportant part,
   Prating of love and knowing only lust,
Nursing eternity within his heart,
   Nor dreaming that his destiny is dust.

All this is blasphemy. Before the worlds began
   The Word that was with God purposed to be made
                                  Man.

THOUGHTS IN A MINUTE'S SILENCE BEFORE A
FOOTBALL MATCH: NOVEMBER 23rd, 1963

The simple, godless people grieve,
  And blindly in their grieving pray
That He in whom they don't believe
  Will wipe their fears away;
Assailing with instinctive prayer
  The God they do not think is there.

The fellow in the football crowd
  Stands in his thousands in the rain,
Silent and reverent and bowed
  And lifts his heart – in vain?
Is it in vain they rise today,
  The prayers of men who do not pray?

The common catalogue of doubt
  Does duty for the working day,
But when disaster finds us out
  What is there it can say?
Thus, then we lift our streaming eyes
  For comfort to the emptied skies.

The half-forgotten things we need,
  For we in ways of woe have trod,
The strength of our neglected creed
  And our abandoned God;
The comforts we conceive to be
  Established in eternity.

For him who lies in Dallas dead,
   And more for her who lives bereaved,
Our simple childish prayers are said
   As though we still believed.
The thing we hope but cannot prove
   We apprehend because we love.

NO ROOM

No room.
There was a handful of wise men, it's true,
Who brought their gifts; some simple shepherds, too,
Who heard the angels sing and made their way
To the poor stable where the Saviour lay.
But for the rest? Well, men were much the same
As now they are – when the Redeemer came.
Like us, of course, within the inn they made
Room for the merchants (always room for trade),
Room for the soldiers, for there has to be
A proper measure of security;
Room for the priests – observed in moderation
Religion is of profit to the nation;
Room for the greed that turns the poor away
And welcomes only people who can pay;
Room for the compromise, that will not quite
Drive an expectant mother into night,
But thinks a stable will suffice for her:
No need to sacrifice a customer.
So every year we pay – we never fail –
Lip-service to the Xmas fairy-tale:
The things that might be, mixed with things that are
Like sleigh-bells – jingling on the Jaguar,
Religious echoes on the radio;
Pale prayers that raise a sentimental glow,

God rest you merry, Christmas brings good cheer,
And herald angels singing – once a year
O come, ye faithful; join with us and praise
The climax of a hundred shopping days.

Was it a dream? Two thousand years are fled
And still we keep for God a cattle-shed.
He cannot harm us there, confined and pent
And insulated by our sentiment.
God in a story, tinsel, pretty-pretty,
Shut up in David's royal, vanished city.

Then, having loved too little and in vain,
Back to the market we can turn again.
Back to our trade, our battles, near and far,
And make for God the road to Golgotha.
No room.

AT A FAREWELL

God be with you till we meet again,
   May he through the days direct you;
   May he in life's storms protect you;
God be with you till we meet again.

God be with you till we meet again;
   And when doubts and fears oppress you,
   May his holy peace possess you.
God be with you till we meet again.

God be with you till we meet again;
   In distress his grace sustain you;
   In success from pride restrain you;
God be with you till we meet again.

God be with you till we meet again.
   May he go through life beside you,
   And through death in safety guide you;
God be with you till we meet again.

PENITENCE

Creator of the earth and skies,
  To whom the words of life belong,
Grant us thy truth to make us wise;
  Grant us thy power to make us strong.

Like theirs of old, our life is death,
  Our light is darkness, till we see
Th' eternal Word made flesh and breath,
  The God who walked by Galilee.

We have not known thee: to the skies
  Our monuments of folly soar,
And all our self-wrought miseries
  Have made us trust ourselves the more.

We have not loved thee: far and wide
  The wreckage of our hatred spreads,
And evils wrought by human pride
  Recoil on unrepentant heads.

For this, our foolish confidence,
  Our pride of knowledge and our sin,
We come to thee in penitence;
  In us the work of grace begin.

Teach us to know and love thee, Lord,
  And humbly follow in thy way.
Speak to our souls the quickening word
  And turn our darkness into day.

RETRO-PSYCHOANALYSIS

'Alice on T V not for the young.' – Headline in *The Guardian*.
'There is an enduring melancholy that outlasts the fun.'
                                                    Jonathan Miller.

The learned man relaxed and smiled
And turned to entertain a child.
He took her gently by the hand
And led her into Wonderland,
And myriads have followed there
And thought it fun to breathe the air,
And never knew how wrong they were.
For now a new, enlightened age
Pontificates upon the page;
Now the informed psychologist
Proclaims the truth our fathers missed
And posthumously preaches on
The bleak subconscious of the Don.
In vain that complicated man
Squirms on his couch Elysian.
The probing finger finds what's hid
In that unpenetrated Id,
Brands schizophrenic on his brow
And Lewis doesn't Carol now.
The tale is tragic for, it seems,
Under the surface of his dreams
The hapless cleric brooded much
On Malcolm Muggeridge and such.
(If that's what he was getting at
By Jabberwock and things like that,

The truth is not – I quite agree –
Fit for the little ones to see.)
The fact, I think, is otherwise.
Somewhere beyond the eternal skies
The Immortals fight for breath enough
To laugh at this pretentious stuff.

DEUTERO – JABBERWOCK

'Twas tillich and the neo-fog
   Did float and fettle o'er the Cam;
All flimsy was the theologue
   And gurgled as he swam.

The Bultmana and the Bezzantine
   Ancestral voices – uttered doom,
And heard from Woolwich voices nine
   Bonhoeffing in the gloom.

The Church's turn had come to burn.
   Encircled by Teutonic names,
And on the stone a Kingly Dean
   Was viddling by the flames.

Professors of emphatic size
   Peruse the much bismatered book
And calmly demythologize
   The grimy pentateuch.

DIRECTION OF LABOUR

When Homer used to smite his lyre
   And sing the lays that Greece enjoyed,
Did Governmental types inquire
   If he was gainfully employed?
Or did they ostracize the bard
Because he had no union card?

When Gloriana ruled the State
   And hearts were proud and heads were high,
Did nobles wonder in debate
   If Spenser was a butterfly;
If Jonson earned the means to live
And whether Shakespeare was a spiv?

O hero, on your lonely height,
   Upon your column's lofty brow,
What think you of the signal light
   That lesser men are flashing now?
'England directs that every man
Should bow the neck to those who plan.'

Yet Englishmen may still be free
   If English hearts and spirits will it,
And we shall live the day to see
   When every ballot finds its billet.
Then labour too, may be directed –
Not to the place that it expected.

ABERSOCH

All the élite prefer to meet at Abersoch,
That's where the best people go;
   The people in society who really count the most,
   Have hitched the boat behind the Jag
   And are heading for the coast:
   And those who rate as sailors of status
   Come from near and far,
   And together get with the yachting set
   In the Lleyn Peninsula:
   For the Barbecue of the harbour crew
   Is a madly gay affair;
   And you simply must meet the upper crust
   Who will be assembled there –
   Oh, Abersoch's where the best people go!

RECIT

Some people seem to find that it meets their recreational needs to
dress up in tweeds; and thus apparelled with shot-guns single and
double-barrelled, they shoot much and carouse more on a grouse
moor, but for me this would be of no avail: give me sail! Give me
sail!

VERSE 2

All the élite prefer to meet at Abersoch,
That's where the best people go;
   It is true there are some sailors who have fallen by the way,

And are slumming at Beaumaris or perhaps Trearddur Bay –
Or they find their heaven at Morfa Nefyn
Or bask at Borth-y-gest;
But those who know the place to go
Know Abersoch is best!
They go in hoards to the Norfolk Broads
To mess about in a boat,
But here you'll meet all the sailing élite
The cream of the creatures afloat –
Oh, Abersoch's where the best people go!

RECIT

Oh it's rough among the rocks when you're hunting for the fox and
you'll catch him only by an awful fluke: but there's nothing we won't
suffer with the Fox that's known as Uffa, and you'll get an extra
fillip with the Duke!

VERSE 3

All the élite prefer to meet at Abersoch,
That's where the best people go;
Some go to Aberdaron in their yachting rig and cap,
But it might as well be Butlin's, it's right off the social map;
By the flowing sea where the wind is free
And everything else is not,
If you have got an expensive yacht you belong to this favoured
spot.
There are those who mock at Abersoch
They've not attained it yet –
For the favoured folk of Abersoch
Are a most exclusive set –
Oh, Abersoch's where the best people,
All the specially dressed people,
Gracious living, abreast people,
Abersoch's quite the most on the coast!

THOUGHTS ON A CHRISTMAS PRESENT

(To be sung at bedtime and made to last as long as possible.)

Once my tiny feet were frozen,
Now, I'm glad to say they're not,
For a present has been chosen
Guaranteed to keep them hot!
    Hot, hot, extremely hot,
    Red and Rubber Water Bot
    Of my very own I've got.
        Hallelujah!

Who is there on earth, I wonder, would
Give me such a friend in need?
Christopher and Judy Underwood
Who are very kind indeed.
    By their bounty I have got
    Rubber, Red and Super-hot,
    Yes, I've got a – you know what!
        Hallelujah!

FOR THE MAYOR OF COLWYN BAY

Where'er I roam by land or foam
　　Where'er my lot is cast,
The strip of coast I cherish most
　　Will call me back at last.
Each Northern-Welsh remembered name
　　Rings in my mind for aye the same.

Can her glories be hid? No. The fame of Llandudno
　　The pens of the poets rehearse.
In the valley of Clwyd an elderly Druid
　　Is writing an epic in verse.
And in Betws-y-Coed they are fully employed
　　In preserving the wonder of Wales.
They are building a road on the summit of Snowdon
　　When Beeching puts paid to the rails.

I dream of Myfanwy the Queen of Deganwy
　　For ever the Queen of my heart,
(Or was it Anharrog, the doll from Dolgarrog?
　　I never could tell them apart.)
What beauty's like that in the town of Prestatyn!
　　It shines in my memory still,
With the caravans splendid, sublimely extended
　　Enhancing the sunshine of Rhyl.

Those I have loved, yet lovelier far than they
I sing the majesty of Colwyn Bay.

.   .   .

If you come to Colwyn Bay you are almost sure to stay,
People visit for a fortnight but they never go away.
Our humble civic centre will delight you as you enter –
It's a beauty – and the residents are privileged to pay.
You can take a cup of tea in the café by the sea
And observe the joys of sailing where the wind at least is free;
Or from early morn till dark live it up in Eirias Park
And the night life's Continental, reminiscent of Paree!
There's a post that points to Penrhos and another signpost too
Which you'd think denoted Rydal but it says it's 'to the Zoo';
But it doesn't matter much, for either place is such
That some interesting specimens the visitor can view.
Though the Odeon is empty and the golfers all are gone
To fresh delights on Colwyn Heights our souls are marching on:
Though the future's not so fair as the past, we are aware,
Now that Mr Fisher's finished with the office of the Mayor.

Extracts from

The Batsman's Bride

An Operetta in One Act

AUTHOR'S NOTE
This is a kind of respectful parody of the immortal Gilbert and Sullivan. The dialogue is deliberately stilted and should be slightly 'ham'. But the songs should be taken seriously and sung straight.

FROM THE OPENING CHORUS OF VILLAGE MAIDENS
Here we hymn the praise of cricket
    Queen of field and lea,
And prepare our choicest wicket
    For the M C C.
For their coming all prepare,
Cows are driven from the square.

GRACE (THE SQUIRE'S DAUGHTER)
Ah, my simple companions, you may well rejoice for your hearts are carefree, but mine is full of grief.

CHORUS
Why? What is the matter?

GRACE
The matter? My father has discovered my love for George Cowshott and has vowed that I shall never marry a man who is not a member of the M C C.

CHORUS
Oh!

GRACE
Yes. He has sworn to bestow my hand on Cyril Straightbat, the Captain of the M C C team which is to play the village this afternoon.

221

(i) Sir Roderick Celluloid
   Is madly keen on cricket;
His riches he's employed
   In perfecting our wicket.
He cares not for success or fashion
Cricket is his consuming passion.

(ii) When first he looked on me
   A tiny, female baby;
'Though but a girl' said he
   'A batsman's bride she may be.'
His eyes with true devotion glistened
'Grace', he said, 'she shall be christened.'

(iii) I've learnt in Cricket's school
   In spite of deepest feeling,
Against the Umpire's rule
   There may be no appealing;
In pleasure's paths I may not linger
But bow to the Umpirial finger.

(iv) So now, though woman grown
   And not devoid of beauty,
I may not choose my own
   But take the path of duty;
Whate'er it may be I must stick it,
To disobey would not be cricket.

.   .   .

FROM THE CHORUS OF VILLAGE CRICKETERS
You may think that we are weak
In refinement and technique
   And we're certainly not studious of style;
But bowl us a half-volley

Or a full-toss and, By Golly!
   We will hit it for a quarter of a mile.

· · ·

SONG OF THE VILLAGE CAPTAIN (GEORGE COWSHOTT)

(i) When I was a little, tiny boy,
       (Dew on the wicket and shine on the ball);
    My father's pride, my mother's joy,
       (Willow in the woods is the King of them all).
    They all had hopes that I should be
    A great, big shot at the top of the tree,
    But nobody knew my secret dream
    One day to be captain of the village team.

(ii) Some get lands and some get gold,
        (Dew on the wicket and shine on the ball);
     Some get fame and all get old,
        (Willow in the woods is the King of them all).
     But hardly anyone finds that he
     Has really climbed to the top of the tree,
     So I'm glad that I dreamed my humble dream
     And find myself captain of the village team.

· · ·

THE VILLAGE UMPIRE'S SONG

(i) I'm the instrument of justice and the symbol of authority,
    At times I may be biassed, but I'm just to the majority;
    The ancient laws of cricket I impartially administer
    And show no fear or favour to the virtuous or sinister.
    You may think that my decision is a sensible or silly 'un,
    But if I lift my finger you are back in the pavilion;
    I do not want opinion or the votes of the majority,
    I *am* the game's dictator and I've absolute authority.

(ii) It is not in human nature to observe complete legality,

223

I *may* sometimes depart from absolute impartiality;
When living in a village feudal obligations trouble you –
It goes against the grain to give the Squire out l.b.w.
And when a fierce opponent moves the score at an improper rate
If the Vicar hits his pads – well, it is easy to co-operate;
But though I may be partial to a privileged minority
I *am* the game's dictator and I've absolute authority.

(iii) If an enemy fast bowler threatens dangerous velocity,
I frequently no-ball him with unspeakable ferocity:
I'm sometimes plagued with deafness – just a passing disability,
But on the whole you'll find I deal out justice with celerity
To our team with reluctance, to the foemen with severity,
At times I may seemed biassed, but I'm just to the majority,
I *am* the game's dictator and I've absolute authority.

.   .   .

THE RADIO COMMENTATOR

Well, here we are on the village green at Cattlecud. I wish you could all be here to see the national game played in a typically English setting. It's a lovely day. The sky is blue with that deep and cloudless blue which we like to associate with an English summer when we get the chance (*rather forced laughter in which the Voice joins*) and the green of the grass is of a quality that no artist could depict. The ground is crowded to capacity; there must be quite three hundred people here, wouldn't you say Rex?

VOICE

Yes, John.

COMMENTATOR

Thank you very much, Rex. I just asked Rex here for his estimate of the crowd and he agrees with me that there must be quite 300 people here. Well, you'll all want to know what the state of the game is. The MCC won the toss and batted first and they are all out for 142, of which their captain, Cyril Straightbat, made 84. A very fine innings, wasn't it Rex?

VOICE

Yes, John.

COMMENTATOR

Thank you very much Rex. Well, we all think here that 142 is a winning score on this wicket. We have had a look at it during the tea interval and we've all agreed that it's what you might call a sporting wicket. I'll ask Arthur to tell you about it. I've just been saying that we think it's a bit sporting.

ARTHUR

Thank you very much, John. Yes, I've just been looking at the wicket and I should describe it as distinctly sporting. There are one or two holes in it and I noticed when the MCC were batting that the village fast bowler managed to make one or two bump out of the batsman's reach. So I think that Straightbat may prove rather difficult to play. I don't want to commit myself, because you never know what will happen in cricket, but I should say that, unless the Cattlecud batsmen manage to stay in on this very sporting wicket against the fast bowling of Straightbat, then this game will end in a win for the MCC. But I may be wrong, of course, and for the sake of the local side, who are a very fine, keen lot, I hope that I am. That's all I've got to say, I think, John.

COMMENTATOR

Thank you very much, Arthur.

.   .   .

SIR RODERICK (THE SQUIRE)

My dear fellow, Cattlecud has never beaten the MCC and we're not likely to make a score like that on this wicket. They've got a very fast bowler you know.

GEORGE

The faster the bowler the faster he shall go to the boundary.

SIR RODERICK

I like your spirit, my boy, but it's hopeless you know. Still, I'm sure you'll put up a good show.

GEORGE

I must go and put my pad on. I'll come back, Grace, and give you the chance to wish me luck before I go in.

. . .

GRACE

Ah, here is George in pad and gloves and with a bat in his hand. How calm and brave he looks. Good luck, George!

GEORGE

Excuse my glove, Grace, I have often gone to the wicket for the sake of the village, but today I shall be batting for your sake. It may be that after today I must go out of your life for ever, but I'll play an innings which you shall remember as long as you live.

GRACE

I will remember it, be it short or long. Even a duck of yours is more precious to me than the century of another.

. . .

[*Duet: George and Grace*]

GEORGE

When evening shadows slant across the green
    And evening breezes beautify the air,
The haunting echoes of what might have been
    Visit the memory and linger there;
All that we have done fades away,
Melts in the evening shades away;
The tale of failure and success is told,
All that the fates have sent to me,
    All that the game has meant to me
Lives, though the final over has been bowled.

GRACE

So when life's evening falls, though far apart
    We rove, and I perchance must walk alone,
You shall abide unfading in my heart
    And all the happiness we two have known;
All else Time's storms may break away.

226

This he can never take away;
Till the last story of our days is told
    All that your love has lent to me,
    All that your self has meant to me
Lives, when life's final over has been bowled.

.   .   .

TWO SOLILOQUIES BY THE VILLAGE UMPIRE

(i) If William Shakespeare wanted, in a play
    A dozen years or so to pass away,
    He had a Chorus, in between the acts
    To put the audience wise about the facts.
    He simply said, 'A dozen years have gone',
    The audience nodded and the play went on;
    And that, if it is all the same to you
    Is what we in this play propose to do.
    Imagine, then, and you'll allow, perhaps
    An hour and twenty minutes to elapse.
    So come we to the climax of our scene
    And I'll return you to the village green.

.   .   .

(ii) L.b. or not l.b. – that is the question,
    The bowler's made a very firm suggestion:
    I must reply with judgment and precision
    For everything depends on my decision.
    The umpire's ruling is as sure as death,
    The village waits and nature holds its breath.
    Though carefully I weigh the evidence
    It would be wrong to keep them in suspense;
    My verdict I must very soon be stating,
    The village waits – I must not keep it waiting,
    Lend me your ears and hear what I decree,
    I am a plain, blunt man as you can see,
    I make no speeches as some others do,

I do my duty and my words are few,
I heard your question; there's no need to shout
And my decision is – it is NOT OUT.

COMMENTATOR

The umpire has given the batsman not out and the last over has been called. And Straightbat, the MCC captain and fast bowler, is going to bowl the last over to Cowshott, the village captain, who has made 70 not out. The village are exactly 29 behind so all Cowshott can do is to try to keep the bowling and keep his end up for this over. Straightbat is running up to bowl now. He takes a long run but he should reach the wicket in a few minutes. He's getting nearer with every step that he takes, isn't he, Rex?

VOICE

Yes, John.

COMMENTATOR

Thank you very much, Rex. He's very near now. He's swinging his arm; he's bowling now: he's bowled!

[*Applause.*]

COMMENTATOR

That was a very good shot. He just got the edge of his bat to it – he's extraordinarily good off the edge – and lifted it over the slips for four. It bounced just short of third man and bounded over his head into the hedge; 'strordinary shot, wasn't it, Rex?

VOICE

Yes, John.

COMMENTATOR

Straightbat's got the ball again and he's running up to bowl; a shorter run this time. He's there; he's bowled. (*Bang. Applause.*) Good gracious it's a six. Cowshott has just hit the second ball of the last over for a six. That was a yorker on the leg-stump. George just took one pace back and two paces to his right, thus making it a half volley on the off, and drove it over the screen. 'Strordinary shot, wasn't it, Rex?

VOICE

Yes, John.

COMMENTATOR

Thank you very much, Rex. Well, they've retrieved the ball and given it back to the bowler and here comes Straightbat again, swinging his arm over and over. He's bowled. (*Bang. Applause.*) It's a good shot, a very good shot; it's a four. That ball was rather wide of his legs and he just swung at it one-handed, like a tennis player with his backhand, and it went to the boundary like a bullet off the back of the bat. 'Strord . . .

VOICE

Yes, John.

COMMENTATOR

Straightbat's taking an even longer run and he's starting to swing his arm even earlier. He's running at a terrific speed. I'll just get Rex to give you his rate.

VOICE

Thank you, John. In-out. One-out. Two-out.

COMMENTATOR

Thank you very much, Rex. He's there – he's bowled. (*Bang. Applause.*) It's a six. Yes, a six. A remarkable shot. Never saw one like it in my life. That ball was rather short of a length and George simply went down on his knees and hit it over his head and the wicket-keeper's for six.

VOICE

'Strordinary shot, John, wasn't it?

COMMENTATOR

Yes, Rex. Well, things are really looking interesting. Cattlecud have now scored 133 for nine wickets, so they need ten runs to win with two balls to go. Incidentally George Cowshott has made 90, so he wants ten, too. Well, here's Straightbat again, looking a little tired, but running very well. He's bowled. Ah, it's the slower one, but it will reach the batsman quite soon, I think. Yes, it's there now. (*Bang. Applause.*) Cowshott didn't quite get hold of that, but he's hit it into that bed of nettles just wide of mid-on: they'll probably manage to run four while the fieldsman is putting his gloves on. Yes, I thought so: a smart bit of fielding, but they've run four. The score is now 137 and Cowshott has made 94. With one ball to go the village need six to win and their captain needs six for his century. The silence here is uncanny: listen: you can almost hear it.

[*A terrific voice, near the mike, shouts:* "it 'im for six, George'.]

Straightbat's taking a tremendous run this time. It'll be some time before he gets to the wicket. He's obviously going to give 'em all that he's got. Here he comes, running with a beautifully easy action. Good Heavens! Cowshott's running too. He's running down the wicket to meet the bowler. Straightbat's bowled!

[*A crash, followed by terrific cheering.*]

It's a six, it's a six! He's won the match. He hit it straight from the bowler's hand and it went up to a terrific height – in fact it hasn't come down yet.

COMMENTATOR AND VOICE

'Strordinary shot, wasn't it?

COMMENTATOR

Here comes the ball, right above the box here. Good night!

.   .   .

Finale

GRACE

We will start as man and wife.

BOTH

The Batsman and his Bride;

GEORGE

On a partnership for life.

BOTH

The Batsman and his Bride;

GRACE

In a matrimonial scene

GEORGE

White will grace the village green,

BOTH

And the sun will shine serene

Upon the Batsman's Bride.

CHORUS

Let the bells in concert ring
   To greet the Batsman's Bride,
Let the happy people sing
   To greet the Batsman's Bride;
Though the skies were overcast
All the threatening clouds have passed,
Yes, the sun will shine at last
   Upon the Batsman's Bride.

The Headmaster's Daughter

or

The Upright Usher

This work was written to commemorate an almost incredible piece of bureaucracy in 1950. The Government decreed that no child should be allowed to sit for the General Certificate of Education, whatever his abilities might be, until he had reached the age of 16. The controlling date was originally named as September 1st. After a great deal of debate it was ponderously announced that children born on September 2nd would be deemed to have completed their sixteenth year on September 1st. Traces of this extraordinay affair still remain. Headmasters are required to sign a statement on the G.C.E. entry form to the effect that any candidates under that age of 16 are good candidates and that it is desirable for them to sit for the examination. This annual insult is inflicted on the teaching profession to save the faces of stupid legislators whose measure collapsed in ridicule after only a year or two.

It is to the memory of those politicians that we dedicate this work; but for them it would never have been written.

Duet for Boy and Girl

1

You're 1066, you're the Scots and the Picts,
You're all the ages in hist'ry's pages,
You're Hector, Lysander and great Alexander,
You're my permanent date.
You're Alfred the Cake, Raleigh and Drake,
Abel and Cain, you're Philip of Spain,

You're sailors in numbers like old man Columbus,
You're my permanent date.
You are all my past and all my future as well,
You are all the secrets I am trying to tell;
You're Aaron and Moses, the Wars of the Roses,
You're Frederick the Great, Henry the Eight,
You're Abraham Lincoln and all I can think on,
You're my permanent date.

2

You're sugar and cream, you're a beautiful dream,
Sunset and dawn, you're poppies in corn,
You're the breeze in the trees and the knees of the bees
You're everything I love.
You're the sky summer brings, you are music that swings,
Silver and gold, a building that's old,
You're a tune that a coon sings in June 'neath the moon,
You're everything I love.
You are all my past and all my future as well,
You are all the secrets I am trying to tell;
You're clothes that are smart, you're the latest in art,
Refreshing to drink, you're a coat that is mink,
You are summer on Bredon, you're Anthony Eden,
You're everything I love.

The Song of Daniel the Delinquent

Who is it that sniffs and that spits in the street?
   Daniel the daring delinquent.
Who is it puts pins on the pedagogue's seat?
   Daniel the daring delinquent.
Who shatters the windows when no-one is by
And when he is caught doesn't scruple to lie?
Who is it? It's me, or more properly, I!
   Daniel the daring delinquent.

236

Duet for Boy and Girl

1

I thought that love would be for ever young,
   That beauty lived for aye and could not die;
I thought the songs that you and I have sung
   Would echo through the years eternally.
I dreamed that happiness could not decay –
How foolish to believe what poets say!
Ah! Well-a-day!
How foolish to believe what poets say!

2

So has it ever been, from that far day
   When Helen's beauty launched a world of woe,
As Tristan from his love was torn away,
   As fortune laughed at hapless Romeo;
So must all hopeful lovers ever be
The sport of mocking fate eternally.
Ah! Woe is me!
The sport of mocking fate eternally.

3

We thought that love would be for ever young,
   We dreamed that beauty never would decay,
We trusted in the poet's lying tongue;
   How foolish to believe what poets say!
So shall all hopeful lovers ever be
The sport of mocking fate eternally.
Ah! Woe is me!
The sport of mocking fate eternally.

Hear me now as I recite
This your sacred regulation:
Tell me if I get it right.
It is writ, as I remember,
Only students may appear
Who the first day of September
Consummate their sixteenth year.

RECIT

Yes, yes, that is the relevant regulation
For the General Certificate of Education.
But a more elastic order
Followed from the Ministry,
So that people on the border –
Line should justly treated be.
Those who on September Second
End their sixteenth year of age
Shall be deemed, it says, or reckoned
To have reached the proper stage.

RECIT

Yes, yes, it is quite true, with vision splendid
That very same concession we extended.
So it is that down the sink went,
I am happy to proclaim
Plots of Daniel the Delinquent
'Gainst a fair, unsullied name.
Mr Sprinter's brave confession
He may happily unsay:
Qualified for your concession
He was born upon that day.

DANIEL

Ask him how old he was when he took his General Certificate.

MINISTER

Well, Mr Sprinter? (*Pause.*)

HEAD

Come on, Sprinter. Speak out!

SIDNEY

Lord Thunderbolt – Headmaster – Ursula – this is indeed a terrible revelation. I have to confess that it is true that I did indeed sit for my General Certificate before I had completed my sixteenth year.

ALL

O horror!

HEAD

My boy, this is a shocking admission that you have made. Your whole career is indeed, as has been said, rooted in dishonest practice. Strictly speaking you have not taken the Certificate, has he, Minister?

MINISTER

Certainly not. It follows that, strictly, he has not obtained exemption from the Previous Examination, and therefore he is not, strictly speaking, a Graduate of Cambridge University nor, still speaking strictly, a qualified teacher within the meaning of the Act. He is not entitled to receive the Burnham Scale for qualified teachers nor the pension and other benefits which go with that munificent remuneration.

HEAD

Sprinter, I am reluctantly compelled to dismiss you from my staff. Never shall it be said that Co-ed College entrusted its pupils to unqualified men. I need hardly add that you cannot hope to support my daughter on the salary of an unqualified teacher. Your engagement is at an end. Have you anything to say?

SIDNEY

Nothing, sir. I will not add defiance, nor any attempt at self-justification, to the offence which I have committed against you, against your family, against the School and – O insupportable shame – against the Ministry of Education. Can you ever forgive me, Ursula?

URSULA

I can forgive, Mr Sprinter, but I cannot dissociate myself from what

239

my father has said. I have been brought up all my life to regard loyalty to the Ministry and its regulations as the foundation of all virtue. I will remember the song that I learned at my mother's knee when the age limit was first introduced in 1950.

[*Sings*]

Sing a song of sixteen, that's the magic age:
No examinations prior to that stage.
Though my teachers say that I was fit a year ago,
The Minister has said I'm not and surely he must know!

LIST OF WORKS

Reason and Imagination
The Apostle's Creed
Some Educational Foundations
What Kind of Education?
The Changing Background of Youth today
A Layman's View
  All published by Epworth Press
The Public Schools and the Future
  Cambridge University Press
The Batsman's Bride (Operetta)
  Oxford University Press
Goodbye to All That (Operetta)
The Headmaster's Daughter (Operetta)
Speech Day (Three-act Play)
The Parson and the Painter (Three-act Play)
In Wolves' Clothing (One-act Play)
Spare the Rod (Play for Television)
Sauce for the Gander (Story for Radio)
Geoffrey Chaucer (a Translation)
A considerable number of sermons, hymns, parables, fables, stories, papers, verse, etc.
Much satirical verse mostly at the expense of the Establishment
As Editor: 'Under Thirty Speaks for Christ'
  Kegan Paul